Prince Rupert Environmental Society
www.saveourskeenasalmon.org

1365 Overlook Street,
Prince Rupert, BC. V8J 2C7

Book Design and Illustration:
Ken McCormick

Photography:

Michael Ambach
www.mikeambach.com

Yvonne Collins

Moyna MacIlroy
www.raincoastdesigns.com

Editor Luanne Roth

Assistant Editor N. Carol Brown

Grateful acknowledgement is made to Susan Musgrave for permission to reprint three poems from Obituary of Light The Sangan River Meditations, Leaf Press.

Printed in Canada

Cataloguing data available from Library and Archives Canada

ISBN 978-0-9917090-0-7

To order a copy of this book, visit our website at:
www.saveourskeenasalmon.org

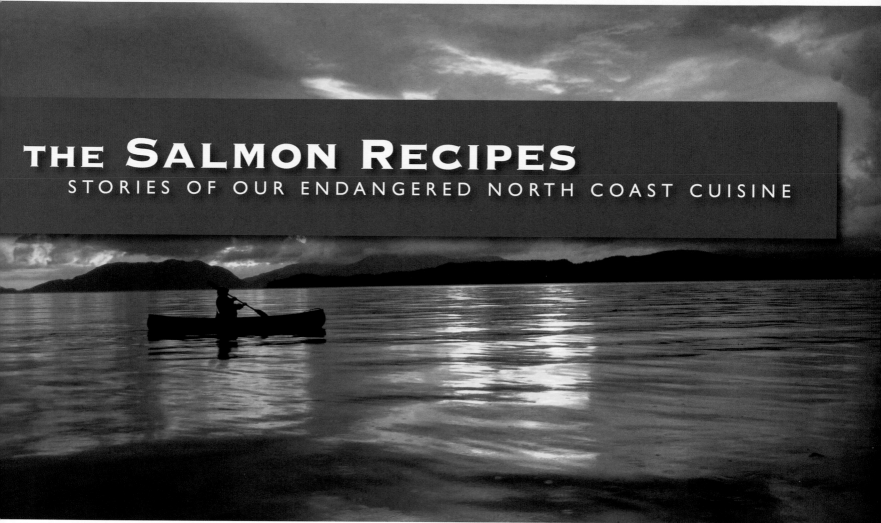

# THE **SALMON RECIPES**
## STORIES OF OUR ENDANGERED NORTH COAST CUISINE

*Photo:* Moyna MacIlroy

Luanne Roth, *Editor*

Ken McCormick, *Design*

**Prince Rupert Environmental Society**
Prince Rupert, *at the mouth of the beautiful Skeena River.*

# CONTRIBUTORS

*Everything in this book has been produced by volunteers.*

**Book Design and Illustration:**
Ken McCormick

**Assistant Editor:**
N. Carol Brown

**Additional editing:**
Susan Henry

**Story and Poem Authors**
Richard Audet
Oliver Bell
Chris Bolten
Dierdre Brennan
Ron Brown Jr.
Sarah Burgess
Henry Clifton
Gary Coons
Daniel Danes
Allan Davidson
Reg Davidson
Robert Davidson
Elvis Davis
Ian Dobson
Rick Haugan

Estrella Hepburn
Cameron Hill
Morgan Hill
Keith Isherwood
Conrad Lewis
Dora Moody
Susan Musgrave
Arnie Nagy
Glenn Naylor
Clarence Nelson
Fanny Nelson
Warren Nelson
Des Nobels
Nicole Robinson
Tom Robinson
Luanne Roth
Leslie Rowlands
Richard Russ Jones
Ocean Rutherford
Milan Stanga
Joy Thorkelson
Shannon Vanderheide
Allan Wilson

**Recipe Authors**
Lou Allison
Roger Arnet
Marty Bowles
N. Carol Brown
Sarah Chi Brown
Yvonne Collins
Karen Fait
Noel Gyger
Mae Jong-Bowles
Jianping's Friend
kalynskitchen.com
Jimmy King
Carole Kristmanson
Doug Laird
David and Kathy Larson
Norma Leakey
Yolanda Malcolm
Jean Martin
Jim Martin
Jeff McDonald
Karen McKinster
Donna McNeil Clark
Eileen Nelson
Shiney O'Neil
Jianping Roth

Luanne Roth
John Rowlands
Leslie Rowlands
Bill Sigurgeirson
Debi Smith
Thomas Spiller
Karen Stepko
Annie Thompson
Shannon Vanderheide

**Photography**
Michael Ambach
www.mikeambach.com

Moyna MacIlroy
www.raincoastdesigns.com
Yvonne Collins
Mae Jong-Bowles
Renata
Marty Bowles
Doug Davis: Prince Rupert Adventure Tours
Steve Milum
Arianne Loranger-Saindon
Ken McCormick
Luanne Roth
Shannon Vanderheide
Eric Yates

**Maps**
Craig Outhet/ *Strait Geomatics*

**Other Contributions**
Amanda Barney
Dane Chauvel
John Crist
Valine Crist
Jennifer Faith Davidson
John Disney
Larissa Goruk
Stephen Johansen
Barbara Kuhl
John Leakey
Laurie Moore
Norm Ostrom
Sunflower Porter
Jennifer Rice
Eloise Robinson
John Roelofs
Mitch Roos
Al Rysstad
Norm Rysstad
Bill Smith
Gerald Stewart
Cheryl Ypma

# INTRODUCTION

This collection of recipes, stories, poems, and photographs comes from north coast people concerned about proposed oil tankers on our waters.

*The Prince Rupert Environmental Society* through its volunteers and supporters has produced this book to share a firsthand experience of the coastal ecosystem: the richness of the area, the value of the vast timeless supply of nutritious salmon, the communities with their personalities, histories and culture and the beauty, danger and wild strength of the winds and waves.

We hope that as you come to understand who we are, you will join us in preserving the spirit of our land and our future.

— Luanne Roth, *editor*

*Photo: Michael Ambach*

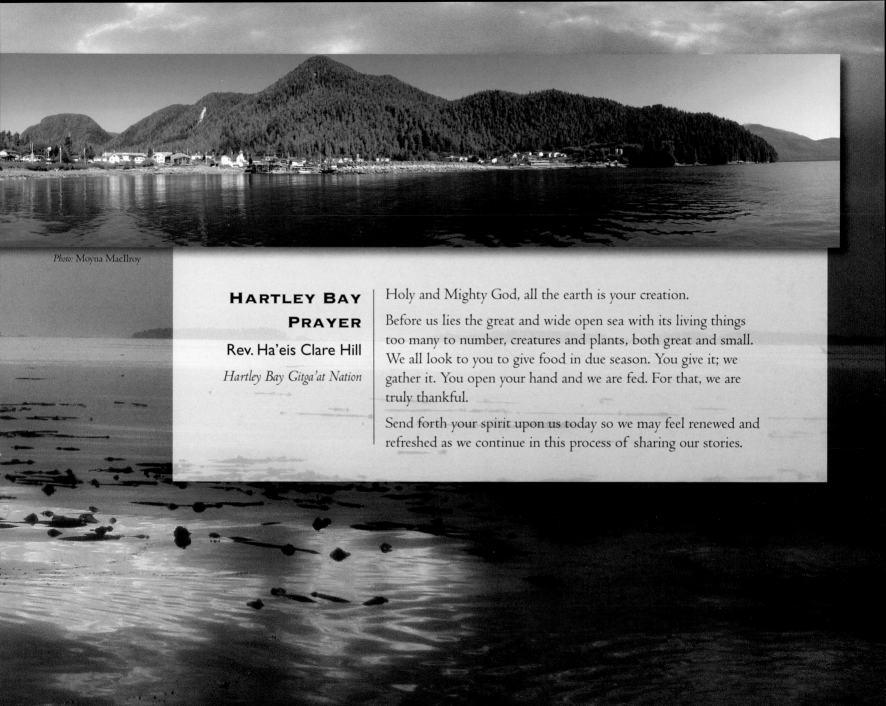

Photo: Moyna MacIlroy

## HARTLEY BAY PRAYER

### Rev. Ha'eis Clare Hill

*Hartley Bay Gitga'at Nation*

Holy and Mighty God, all the earth is your creation.

Before us lies the great and wide open sea with its living things too many to number, creatures and plants, both great and small. We all look to you to give food in due season. You give it; we gather it. You open your hand and we are fed. For that, we are truly thankful.

Send forth your spirit upon us today so we may feel renewed and refreshed as we continue in this process of sharing our stories.

## GENERAL CAUTIONS ABOUT SEAFOOD

### Smoking & Pickling

We all know about keeping surfaces clean and keeping fish cold until using. Be especially careful with fish and only cold smoke or pickle fish that you know is of the highest quality. It is best to consult an expert if you are cold smoking for the first time.

### Gathering Clams or Oysters

Wild shellfish can be very dangerous and are often affected by poisonous outbreaks, particularly in the summer. There are safe times, but always check with the experts before gathering.

### Driftwood Fires

Seawater is full of salt. Salt is a combination of sodium and chlorine, which can be delicious on food. But when salt is heated, it breaks down into its parts and the chlorine part combines with organic matter at high heats to form some nasty chemicals. It's safer to go into the bush to gather your beach barbeque firewood. Don't cook with driftwood.

*Photo:* Moyna MacIlroy

# THE NORTH COAST

*Photo:* Michael Ambach

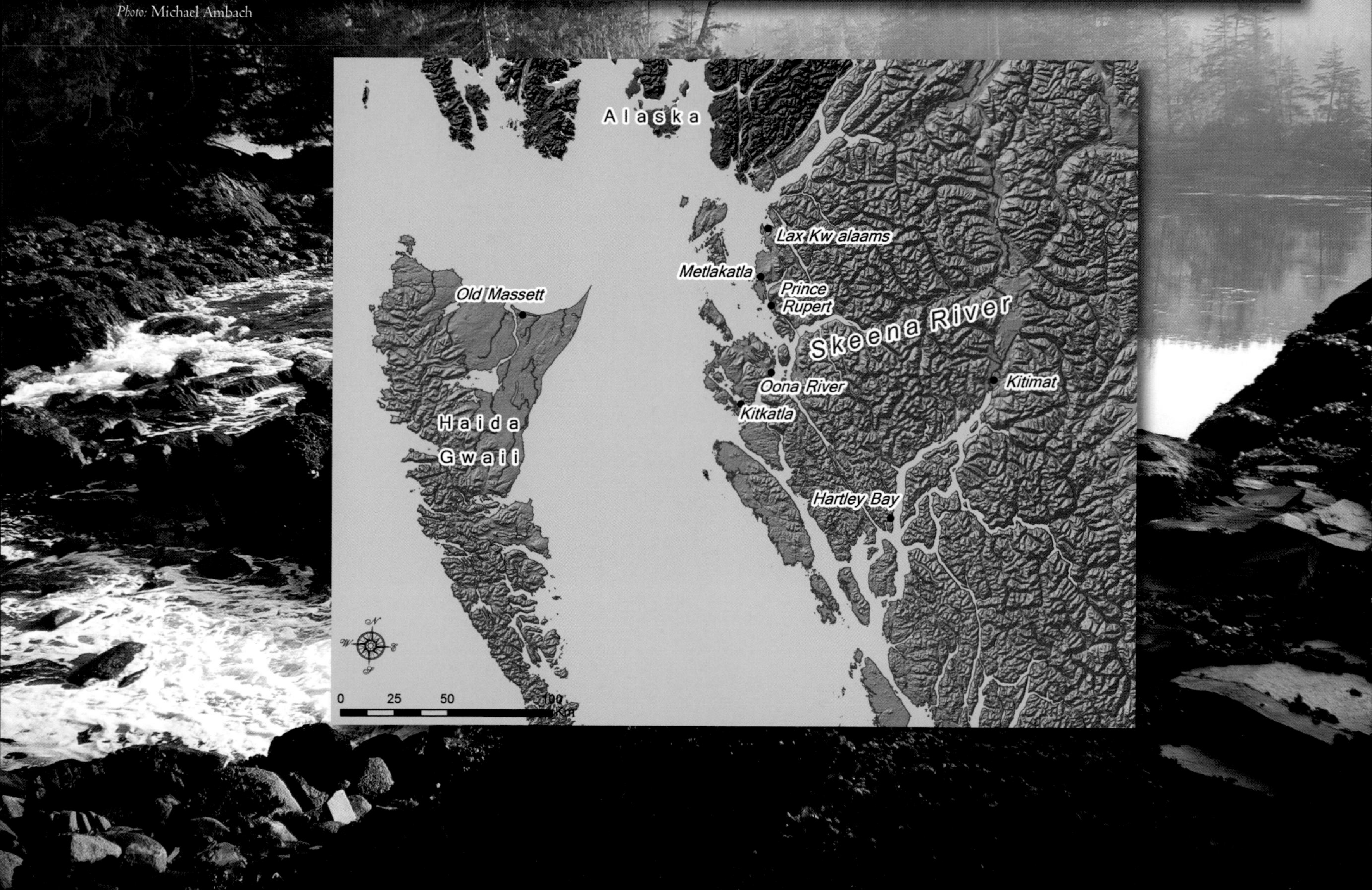
Alaska
Lax Kw alaams
Metlakatla
Prince Rupert
Old Massett
Skeena River
Kitimat
Oona River
Kitkatla
Haida Gwaii
Hartley Bay
N
W
E
S
0
25
50
100
Km

# TABLE OF CONTENTS

## CHAPTER ONE

### Coastal Culture stories

### Traditional and Special Dinners

## CHAPTER TWO

### Seasons of Sharing stories

# TABLE OF CONTENTS

## CHAPTER TWO

## CHAPTER THREE

# TABLE OF CONTENTS

## CHAPTER THREE

## CHAPTER FOUR

### Wild Winds stories

### Party Favorites

# CHAPTER FIVE

**Endless Circle of Salmon stories**

**Everyday Salmon Dishes**

Photo: Moyna MacIlroy

## WHITE BEAR

### Nicole Robinson

*Gitga'at First Nation*

Last year, I took my twin sister out for the first time to Ryorden to see the white bears. She lived in this area a lot of her life and we always just took for granted what was around us.

When I took her to Ryorden, the white bears showed up in about half an hour, I looked at my twin and she was crying. I kind of laughed at her and thought, "Why are you crying?"

It was because she finally got to understand why I go out on the boat every day and she just looked at me and said she will never tease me or bug me about going out on the boat. I told her, "Now you see the beauty in what we see."

## COME FISH WITH ME

### Cameron Hill
Aayawk,
Ha'gwil laxhaand,
and Ka'gwaays

*Hartley Bay*
*Gitga'at*

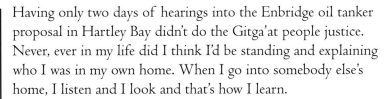

Having only two days of hearings into the Enbridge oil tanker proposal in Hartley Bay didn't do the Gitga'at people justice. Never, ever in my life did I think I'd be standing and explaining who I was in my own home. When I go into somebody else's home, I listen and I look and that's how I learn.

With that, I heard my people that are older than me say, "Come back. You come back." The invitation has been extended for you to go and see some of the beauty that we have in our area. I'll extend that invitation because that's the way that I was taught. I love to fish. You come fish with me; then you'll really learn who I am.

Photo: Yvonne Collins

## ICELANDIC PICKLED SALMON

### Remembered from Bill Sigurgeirson

*This is a must for holiday visitors.*

3 quarts salmon pieces

3 onions

pickling salt or kosher salt

### Pickling Mixture:

10 C white vinegar 5% (don't dilute)

2 C white sugar

½ C brown sugar (add more sugar if desired)

8 T pickling spices

Pick the highest quality fish for pickling; absolutely fresh, frozen at sea or at harbour side. Frozen salmon is best for pickling because a week in a good home or commercial deep freezer takes any worry out of eating uncooked fish.

Partially thaw and filet salmon, remove skin, and cut into bite sized pieces. Soak salmon pieces in a stainless steel pot in the refrigerator for 8 to 12 hours in a mixture of half salt and half water. I turn the mixture every few hours. When brining is complete, thoroughly rinse, changing the cold water many times. Put the drained pieces back in the fridge for an hour to dry, and firm up.

Mix the pickling mixture ingredients in a stainless pot and boil for 20 minutes, stirring occasionally. Cool the mixture down before pouring it over the fish. Slice the onions thin and layer fish pieces and onion into pint jars. After each layer or two, add pickling mixture. Make sure to swish up a good mixture of pickling spices so each jar gets its share. Fill jars and tighten lids.

Refrigerate and turn jars upside down for a day or two during the first week. The pickled salmon is best after a week and easily keeps six weeks or a bit more. Keep refrigerated.

## THEY'RE NOT TAKING US ALIVE

Glenn Naylor

*Prince Rupert*

So anyway, I spent a lot of time kayaking up and down the coast, got to see some really amazing things. I ran into — I think it's a school of grey cod. It was probably about a mile long and from the surface of the water right to the bottom; it was about six fathoms. We jigged, and with no bait on the hook, just pulling the hook up, we caught a fish every time we pulled up. There were that many fish.

We continued on, we kayaked up — no, we canoed up through the islands and ran back into that school of fish and there was a pod of 25 killer whales that were feeding on that particular school of fish. And thank God they were full because we were within 10 or 15 feet of them and the wife asked me why I loaded the rifle. I said "Well, they're not taking us alive". It was pretty scary. But it's the kind of life that's there.

## BITE IT UNCLE

Robert Davidson
Guud sans glans
(Eagle of the Dawn)

*Old Massett*

Our Elders knew the lands and waters like the backs of their hands. I learned this by going halibut fishing with Tsannii Robert Davidson, Sr. He was almost blind when I went fishing with him. Even with his limited vision, he was able to pinpoint where to anchor to fish and where the landmarks were, which are still used today.

When I went jigging for halibut with Tsannii, I learned that the halibut are really uncles to all the Haida people, because these uncles fed us and took care of our families. Tsannii talked to the halibut in Haida and called the halibut uncle. He yelled, "Da.aljiid kaagee!" "Bite it Uncle!"

When he caught the halibut he would talk to it in Haida as he was pulling it up, "Gudangang hl tl'aatsgadii! "Make your mind strong because I'm going to club you!" When he got the halibut onboard he got the new halibut bait, rubbed it into the eyes of the halibut and said, "Remember this; don't just look at the bait. Bite it!" When there were long periods without bites he would say- he would holler, "Don't just look at the bait. Bite it! So I can put food on the table."

## FISH SOUP WITH FINNAN HADDIE ROOTS

### Inspired by Jeff McDonald

1½ C chopped leeks; tender ones or just the tops

pepper

light olive oil or butter

½ lb of smoked blackcod or smoked salmon

(Optional: additional ½ lb of other fish, fresh; lingcod, salmon, halibut, shrimp…)

1 bay leaf

1 large potato in small pieces

½ C each of chopped celery and/or carrots

2 C whole milk

Cook the leeks gently in butter with lots of pepper until they are tender.

While the leeks are taking their time getting soft in the uncovered frying pan get out a large pot. Simmer the bay leaf, smoked fish (fresh goes in later) and potatoes in the milk, but be careful not to let it come to a boil. Add the carrots and celery after the potatoes have cooked a while. Put the leeks in too. Keep it simmering very hot but not boiling.

When the potatoes are starting to soften into the milk add the fresh fish. Hot simmer until the fish is just cooked about ten minutes (shrimp even less).

*Smoking Black Cod in Smokehouse.*

Photos: Michael Ambach & Luanne Roth

If you are using frozen fish, try to get all of the excess moisture out, letting it drain and be sure to pat dry. Put all of the ingredients into a food processor and run for one minute. Stop. Scrape sides of bowl and process for one minute more, or until batter is thick and smooth, and will form nicely on a tablespoon. Chill the batter in the fridge for one hour or longer, then get ready to fry.

Fill a frying pan (I use a stainless steel one) to half full with canola oil. Heat oil on high quickly at first, then reduce down to medium. (Everyone's pan and stove are different). You want a heat that won't brown the fishcakes too quickly. With a tablespoon, scoop out the batter and drop off the spoon one ball at a time into the hot oil. As soon as the balls brown on top, flip over and fry the other side, working quickly.

Transfer the first batch of fishcakes into a pot to steam, (steaming helps to cook the centers and makes them puff up.) I keep a pot on the back burner with a tight fitting lid with about an inch of water on the bottom. When the pot is halfway full up with fishcakes, I take them out and transfer them onto a plate lined with paper towels, and then I start a new batch.

Making fishcakes takes practice, as the quality of the fish can vary. Make sure fresh or frozen that it is of good quality, and free of excess moisture. Good Luck!

2 C fresh cubed lingcod (or I cup lingcod and I cup of halibut)

¾ C whole milk

I egg

2 T potato flour (starch)

I T minced onion

½ t nutmeg

I level T salt

## Red Pepper Aioli

½ red pepper sliced
½ jalapeno pepper chopped
2 sun dried tomato pieces
I garlic clove
½ lemon, juice and zest
3 T fresh cilantro
¼ C mayonnaise
2 T olive oil
Pinch of salt

Put all of the ingredients into a food processor and blend until smooth. Chill until ready to use. (Some delis allow you to buy as many sun dried tomatoes as you want, packed in oil)

# NORWEGIAN FISH CAKES

## Leslie Rowlands

*Here is my grandmother's recipe for traditional Norwegian fishcakes using lingcod that I grew up with. True to the homeland, we tasted the same recipe done up by our relatives on a recent trip to Norway. Norwegians never wasted anything, and my job was to scrape out the flesh from the lingcod cheeks after my Dad had filleted it and he also saved the tongue, a delicacy.*

*The fishcakes are served with a brown gravy which I have included here. Also, for a nice complement, serve a red pepper aioli or buy a ready made hot pepper jelly with pomegranate or mango.*

### Brown Gravy

¼ C flour
I C water
I C low sodium chicken stock
I T butter
½ t nutmeg
Salt and pepper to taste

On the stovetop, brown the flour until light golden brown in a dry stainless steel frying pan or in a heavy stainless steel pot, stirring constantly. Be careful. The flour browns quickly and is very hot. Take the pan off of the heat, and put it back on a cold burner to let it cool down to room temp. While off the heat, slowly add half the water stirring to make a thick paste.

Return pan to the heat and add a little at a time: the other half of the water, chicken stock, butter, nutmeg, salt and pepper. Stir on medium heat to make a smooth gravy.

Photo: Michael Ambach

Photos: Moyna MacIlroy

## LOUIS VUITTON

### Ocean Rutherford

*Prince Rupert*

When visiting friends in Vancouver I often stay in the heart of the city, in Yaletown. I can stay there for a maximum of five days and then my surroundings really start getting to me.

I often think how out of touch the children that grew up there, in urban settings, might be with nature when they are older. The children who grew up in the condos of Yaletown may never need to know how to run a lawnmower. Then again, I may never need to know how to tell the difference between a Louis Vuitton bag and one from the bargain store.

## DRIFT BOTTLES AND MOMMA HUMPBACK

### Morgan Hill

*Hartley Bay*
*Gitga'at First Nation*

One day in fall we went to release bottles which held messages that were going to be used to show the currents and to document how things travel on the water and how fast they move.

As we set our bottles into the water, a momma humpback whale and her baby came alongside the boat we were riding. She passed under the boat, her head came up, her baby played and their eyes met ours. They were massive, but we were in no way threatened.

The two amazing animals stayed with us for over two hours. We watched her and she watched us. This was more than a visit; everybody on that boat knew something big was happening. It was as if the whales knew and we knew. We share the size of the struggle and threat, the difficult road that faces our land, people and identity and our very survival.

## BAKED SALMON WITH LEMON-EGG SAUCE

### Carole Kristmanson

*For special occasions the sauce can be made ahead and the salmon is easily assembled early in the day.*

I salmon

I large chopped onion

2 or 3 sprigs of
fresh rosemary
(or about 2 tsp. dried)

I or 2 bay leaves

20 or so peppercorns

7 or so whole allspice

2¼ t salt

This recipe is suitable for any species of salmon, or even halibut. We like "Spring" the best, but the amounts here are for a 6-7 pound sockeye, head and tail removed. Lay the fish on a large piece of heavy aluminum foil that is 2 ½ times the length of the fish and sprinkle the above ingredients in and around. Fold the foil around the fish with double folds on the top and sides. Place on a rimmed cookie sheet and bake at 350° F for 50 minutes. Let it sit 10 minutes or more before opening the packet.

### lemon-egg sauce:

¼ C butter
¼ C chopped onion
¼ C flour
1¼ C whole milk
¼ C fresh lemon juice
¼ C mayonnaise
I t Worcestershire sauce
1/8 t black pepper
½ t salt
2 chopped hard-boiled eggs

Soften the onion in a small saucepan with the butter over low to medium heat for about 8 minutes. Stir in the flour and simmer for a minute or two before slowly pouring and whisking in the milk until the sauce is smooth. Cook until it is bubbling and thickened. Now, stir in the lemon juice, mayonnaise, Worcestershire sauce, pepper, salt and hard-boiled eggs.

Serve fish and sauce separately.

Photo: Michael Ambach

## CHRISTMAS DRIFT BOTTLE

Shannon Vanderheide

*Oona River*

It was a beautiful, sunny morning and we decided to pack a picnic and head to our favourite local beach for a Christmas day bonfire.

My oldest daughter was running ahead and, when she got to the beach, started screaming with excitement. I saw four humpback whales spouting in the distance and thought that's what all the excitement was. But no; she'd found a message in a bottle. We opened it up and found a message from the drift bottle project.

In the background of all of this message in a bottle excitement, the whales started singing. I couldn't believe our luck. What a Christmas present.

We reported the bottle when we got home and found out that there had been two others reported on the exact same beach. Then it hit me. In the event of an oil spill, we are directly at the end of a very straight Grenville Channel, which could have hundreds of supertankers a year passing it filled with oil.

I also learned that our drift bottle was dropped at Gil Island by a girl named Cassidy from the Hartley Bay School. The drift bottles travelled 94 kilometres in a maximum of 10 days.

*Photo: Shannon Vanderheide*

## KAMABOKO

### Longtime Former Port Edward Japanese Family

*Japanese Fish Cakes — drill required*

4 C salmon (pink, sockeye, spring or chum)

1 egg

½ C sugar

½ C cornstarch

½ C water
+ 1 t dashinomoto
(Japanese soup stock powder)

2 t salt

½ t or so sesame oil

1/3 C chopped green onions

1/3 C grated carrots

Fillet the salmon, remove the skin from fillets. Chop fish into chunks and run through the meat grinder or food processor. Consistency should be fairly fine grind. Then add everything BUT the salt, oil and vegetables to the fish and mix until smooth.

Transfer into a larger pot (I use a stainless steel pot) and beat with a drill. Use your mixer beater on the end of the drill. Add the salt and beat until shiny and elastic. It takes quite a bit of beating, 10 minutes or so. Do not use your mixer as salmon gets very firm when you add the salt.

Before deep frying add some sesame oil and your vegetables. Form into balls (wet your hands as the batter is quite sticky) and deep fry until they float.

*Notes from others who have made Kamaboko:* If you like it sweeter, add a little more sugar; deep fry a couple first and taste. You can double the recipe. You can use a mixer if you have a powerful one. If you make a large batch, you can freeze some of the batter for future use, but once deep fried, the fishcakes don't freeze well. Some add a touch of burdock.

Photos: Michael Ambach & Yvonne Collins

COASTAL CULTURE

Photo: Michael Ambach

COASTAL CULTURE

# LITTLE ESKIMO

## Nicole Robinson

*Gitga'at*

I moved back to Hartley Bay in '97 and was pregnant with my now 14-year old child and that was the start of my learning journey to my culture.

I went to Kiel that year for the first time. That was my second time ever being there in my life and that was when I first learned a lot about my traditional foods that I always took for granted; where it came from and all the hard work that went into the process, such as drying halibut and picking and drying seaweed.

I learned from all the Elders that were there and my mother and father.

They took us out on the boat. They taught us how to cut the fish, how to hang the fish and the whole process until the Elders arrived who also helped us.

My daughter is three years old. We took her for the first time last year and she loves it there. My daughter and her best friend are three years old and they were inseparable in Kiel. They spent the majority of their time down at the beach. Everyone called my daughter "Little Eskimo" because she spent so much of her time in the water.

I want that to always be there for them to know those two will grow up together and always have Kiel there together so they can teach their children and take their children to Kiel.

Photo: Yvonne Collins

*Photo: Michael Ambach*

## SEAFOOD STUFFED SALMON STEAKS

### Jianping's Friend

salmon steaks

shrimp and small scallops (and/or crab meat)

your favorite barbeque sauce (I use smoke BBQ)

maple syrup

salt and pepper

fresh water chestnuts

chopped green onion

parmesan cheese (or ricotta or sour cream)

italian style breadcrumbs

a bit of corn starch

garlic powder

Mrs. Dash Seasoning (optional)

I egg

lemon (or raspberries)

olive oil

Use salmon steaks (or fillet). Marinate with your favorite sauce with an equal amount of maple syrup and some salt and pepper. Marinate for at least 30 minutes but not overnight.

To prepare the stuffing, chop up the shrimp and scallops and most importantly, fresh water chestnuts for enhanced texture. Add the onion, cheese, breadcrumbs, a bit of corn starch, garlic powder and Mrs. Dash Seasoning. Mix I egg into the stuffing. The egg acts as glue to hold things together but cornstarch will do the trick too. I personally like to include the egg as it tastes better but you probably can do without it.

Arrange the stuffing in the center of the steaks. Garnish with a slice of lemon or fresh raspberries on top and drizzle with olive oil. Bake at 400° F for 12-15 minutes or until done. Serve and eat and enjoy with fresh salad, rice or however you like. Good luck.

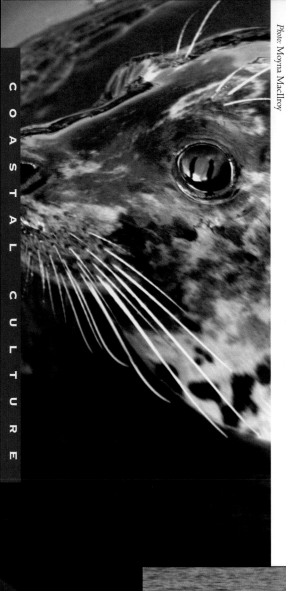

Photo: Moyna MacIlroy

C O A S T A L   C U L T U R E

## OUR REWARD

### Joy Thorkelson

*Prince Rupert*

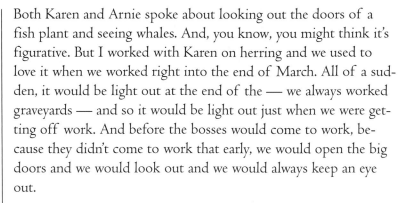

Both Karen and Arnie spoke about looking out the doors of a fish plant and seeing whales. And, you know, you might think it's figurative. But I worked with Karen on herring and we used to love it when we worked right into the end of March. All of a sudden, it would be light out at the end of the — we always worked graveyards — and so it would be light out just when we were getting off work. And before the bosses would come to work, because they didn't come to work that early, we would open the big doors and we would look out and we would always keep an eye out.

Barry Morgan actually, Karen's brother-in-law, it was his job to keep an eye out for those whales coming down the harbour. And we would stop working just to watch them come down the harbour and feed on herring. And that was sort of like our reward every year at the end of herring season.

## RAVEN AND THE BLIND HALIBUT FISHERMAN

### Robert Davidson, Guud sans glans, (Eagle of the Dawn)

*Haida Gwaii*

Raven was flying over the water and he saw the blind halibut fisherman jigging for halibut and Raven, being a prankster, wanted to play a joke on the fisherman, so he dove into the water to look for the halibut hook. In the supernatural realm when we go from the air to the water it's no different. When we enter the water, the water is no different from the air.

So Raven is looking for the halibut hook, he finds it and he pretends to be the halibut and tugs on the hook and the halibut fisherman; he is so excited he has a bite. So he yanks the line to snag the halibut. He yanks so hard that he pulls off Raven's beak. When the blind halibut fisherman pulled up his catch, all he could feel was a real strange object and so at the end of his fishing day he brought it home.

When he was told by the people in the village that it was Raven's beak he hung it up to dry but Raven snuck into the village. He was so embarrassed having lost it that he snuck in to get his beak back.

## CONVERTED EAST COAST CHOWDER

### Jean Martin

*My father was an East Coaster and he taught me at an early age to make traditional East Coast chowder. Born in PEI, he came to BC in 1925 and worked as a telegraph operator in Ayainsh. Today on our north coast I have a variety of wonderful seafood that may be incorporated into the basic chowder.*

1 lb. cod, red snapper, scallops or canned clams

1 lb. white potatoes

1 large onion

2-3 sticks celery

½ lb. good quality bacon, diced

2 T flour

Fry up bacon and set aside, reserving 1 T drippings. Cut your fish or seafood into 1 inch pieces and set aside. Peel and dice potatoes; add chopped onions and celery and cook all the vegetables in salted water (clam nectar is a good addition). Test for doneness by piercing the potatoes with a fork after about 8-10 min.; don't overcook. Add diced bacon to pot. When the vegetables are nearly tender, float seafood on top of the chowder and cook for about 4-5 minutes. When it is just done, thicken with 2 T flour mixed with bacon dripping if necessary.

Photo: Michael Ambach

*Photo: Moyra MacIlroy*

## SANGAN RIVER MEDITATION

### Susan Musgrave

*Haida Gwaii*

A moment ago I heard

a raven speak: *feed me,*

*stay away, come over here,*

*pay attention!* Imagine. Up

until that moment the ravens

and I had not been on speaking terms.

*Photo: Yvonne Collins*

## PROUDEST MOMENTS

### Ocean Rutherford

*Prince Rupert*

Many my age seem quite eager to get out of town these days. In this situation, however, I feel quite proud. I am a fourth generation Rupert-ite. Over a century ago, my great grandparents immigrated to Oona River, which is 40 kilometres south of Prince Rupert on Porcher Island and they came from Sweden.

I've been fed by the ocean my entire life. My favourite seafood is halibut and once I caught an 80-pound halibut on a child's trout rod. It was one of my proudest moments.

The next on my list is sockeye salmon. I'm sure they are some of the healthiest foods on earth.

# CHAMOMILE TEA SALMON WITH TRADITIONAL ACCOMPANIMENTS

## Chef Jimmy King

*Jimmy gave us his "Aroma Therapy Dish" on a visit to the north coast.*

4-6 lbs sockeye salmon fillet

3 T chamomile tea (loose leaf)

3 T lavender honey

2 whole lemons

4 garlic cloves

2 T Piedmont chili pepper (not available paprika)

3 T olive oil

1 T lavender

sea salt and crushed pepper to taste

Clean and debone salmon.

Use 1 cup of water to tea for condensed flavour; for a 10 min. reduction.

Dust paprika over salmon. Sprinkle salt and pepper. Cut and spread garlic evenly (finely diced). Drizzle honey. Rub olive oil to blend these flavors. Pour juice of 1 lemon consistently.

Pre-heat oven to 400° F. Let salmon rest for 20 minutes. Cook salmon on sheet pan for 10 minutes or medium rare. Let rest 5 minutes.

Garnish with lavender, the remaining wheeled lemon over the centre of fish, and the rind of one lemon. Pour condensed tea as sauce around the fish. Serve family style or cut into six ounce portions without skin.

Enjoy for taste and aroma calming.

*Photo: Michael Ambach*

*Photo: Moyna MacIlroy*

## FROM HERE TO THE OTHER SHORE

Reg Davidson,
Skil kaatl'aas,
*(Spirit Weath who is rising)*,
Hlk 'yaan K'ustaan
Sgaanuwee
*(Frog Spirit)*, and
Kiidlajuuwee,
*(the bow of the canoe that
cuts the water in half)*.

*Old Massett*

I'm talking about our territories. I'm talking about Haida Gwaii.

I went online to look at an oil tanker, and the largest one is 1,500 feet in length. It's 415 metres. So I live about the same distance down this road. For me to see the size of it, I visualized that it went from here to the other shore of the inlet. That's the length that boat would be.

*Photo: Michael Ambach*

We have a rediscovery program at Lepas Bay on the northwest tip of Haida Gwaii. Children are taught Haida culture; how to gather seafood and survival skills. They also have the use of canoes, kayaks and do a lot of hiking and playing on the sandy beaches.

Children who attend have memorable experiences. I've had the opportunity to drop off salmon to these kids and I've had the opportunity as well to build platforms out there for them. So I could see the happiness on their faces.

Lepas Bay is around the corner of Perry Pass. The force of the tide running through Perry Pass creates a back eddy into Lepas Bay. Any kind of disaster will wipe out that beautiful spot.

### CHILDREN'S SMILES

**Oliver Bell, Gliii glaa, (Calm Sea)**

*Port Clements*

Photo: Yvonne Collins

Photo: Moyra MacIlroy

## CHAPTER TWO STORIES

First Kill

Own an Onion?

Local Foods

Broker we Were, Better we Ate

True to That, I Do It

A Saviour

Seaweed Shingles

It's Starting to Grow

Good for that Winter

Borrowed a Pressure Cooker

Fish on my Doorstep

Fill our Buckets

My own Berry Pickers!

An Artform

That's Blackcod!

Winter Butter Clams

Sangan River Meditation

Potlatches

## RECIPES

Cedar Planked Salmon Topped
With Dungeness Crab

Chili Grilled salmon with Mango Salsa

Salmon Burgers

Salmon on the Grill with Cheese
and Cracker Spread

Award Winning Olympia Salmon Marinade

Canning Salmon and Halibut

Green Grilled Salmon Belly Dinner Salad

Barbecued Salmon with Teryaki Marinade

Pineapple Express

Scottish Method for Cold Smoked Salmon

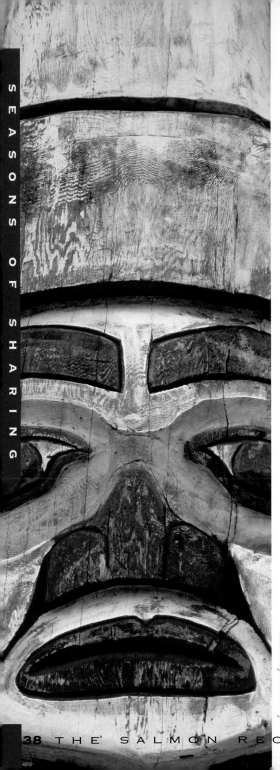

## FIRST KILL

### Warren Nelson, Ama gydem naat

*Kitkatla, Gitxaala*

It's our uncles that take us out on our boat to get our first kill, because our uncles are our fathers also.

And when we get our first kill, our first catch, we take it home and they teach us how to prepare our first kill; how to skin it or how to gut the fish. And when we're done doing that they get us boxes or bags and these boxes or bags are for your aunties and you have to give it out to your auntie.

And that is what I was taught by my grandmother Emma, my gran-gran. When I got back, she taught me this. I was just shocked. I got a big spring salmon. I was so happy, walked up with it, cleaned it and then she said, "You've got to give it all away." And that's what I did.

She gave it to me, I was done cutting it, and she said, "Okay, this is going to your auntie. This is going to our house leader. This is going to Sm'ooygit Hale"— when he was here. And I had to deliver all this fish to these people. And that is a way of our ayaawx and adawx, of our first kills.

## OWN AN ONION?

### Leslie Rowlands

*Prince Rupert*

In the 1970's and 1980's my father Melvin Holkestad, commercial fisherman, would phone from the boat while coming into Port to unload at Prince Rupert Fisherman's CO-OP and ask me quickly, "Leslie, do you own an onion?" And I would have to scramble to produce one, because he would be feeding our table with fresh fish that evening. I never knew if it would be a fresh piece of halibut, sole, salmon, cod or his favourite, brill. For certain whatever we cooked up for dinner would be put into a mash for breakfast, and that's when the humble onion made its statement.

In those days, an onion was enough for flavour. But nowadays I would go looking for a jalapeno pepper, some cherry tomatoes, an orange pepper, some fruity mango and some cilantro to toss up into a salsa, or make a red pepper aioli because fresh fish is such a luxury now, rather than a staple of our diet as it was back then.

*Photo: Moyna MacIlroy*

*Photo: Michael Ambach*

S E A S O N S   O F   S H A R I N G

# CEDAR PLANKED SALMON TOPPED WITH DUNGENESS CRAB

## Shannon Vanderheide

*The cedar adds a lot of flavour to the salmon and the dungeness crab mixture is just decadent!*

1 salmon in 2 fillets

2 T soy sauce

2 C of shucked crab meat

½ C of mayonnaise

2 T grainy mustard

2 cloves of minced garlic

zest of 1 lemon

Take a cedar grilling plank and soak in water for a couple of hours so that it doesn't burn on the barbeque. Pour the soy sauce on the fillets and let sit.

Mix together the crab meat, mayonnaise, mustard, garlic and lemon zest.

Lay the fillets of salmon directly on the soaked cedar plank and top with the dungeness crab mixture. Put the plank with the salmon on a hot barbeque grill and grill it until the fish loses its dark red translucency (about 12 minutes or so).

*Photo: Michael Ambach*

Photo: Moyna MacIlroy

## LOCAL FOODS

### Estrella Hepburn

*Massett, Haida Gwaii*

When I arrived, I had been a vegetarian for 10 years and was buying a lot of tofu at the co-op. But I soon learned from the locals that there was a lot of food that could be gathered and hunted and fished.

We supplement our family's diet with seafood, such as salmon, halibut, clams, scallops, octopus, chitons, mussels, crabs, cockles and seaweed.

My kids are strong and healthy thanks to these local foods… My life revolves around the harvesting, fishing, gathering, storage and preparation of these foods.

## BROKER WE WERE, BETTER WE ATE

### Dierdre Brennan

*Massett, Haida Gwaii*

I have lived my entire life on the west coast of Canada, mostly here on beautiful Haida Gwaii. I raised four children here and even when there wasn't a penny in the bank, we always had food, thanks to the generosity of community members and our own work picking, digging and canning.

We used to joke that the broker we were, the better we ate because that was when the treasures came out; canned fish, clams, deer meat and berries.

## CHILI GRILLED SALMON WITH MANGO SALSA

### Roger Arnet

*Amanda Barney prepared this mouthwatering meal for our photo.*

1½ lbs (750g) salmon fillet, skin on

2 T chili oil (or substitute 2T olive oil plus hot pepper sauce to taste)

2 T lime juice

2 T finely chopped cilantro

1 T grated fresh ginger

2 garlic cloves, minced

Preheat barbeque to medium-high, oil the grill.

Mix together all ingredients except salmon in a small bowl. Reserve 1 T of this mixture to season the salsa (see below). Smear the remaining mixture over the flesh side of the salmon.

Sear salmon, flesh side down for 3 minutes, turn over, cover grill and cook another 7-10 minutes until salmon just flakes when pressed with a fork. (Alternatively, place salmon on grill skin side down and cook, covered, 10-12 minutes.)

### Fresh Mango Salsa

1 tomato diced

1 mango peeled and diced

¼ C chopped green onion

2 T chopped cilantro

1 T reserved chili oil mixture (see above)

salt and freshly ground pepper to taste

Combine just before serving.

*Photo: Steve Milum*

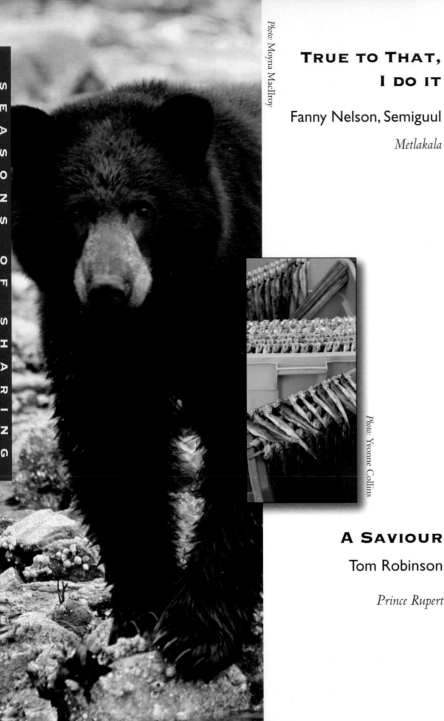

Photo: Moyna MacIlroy

Photo: Yvonne Collins

## TRUE TO THAT, I DO IT

### Fanny Nelson, Semiguul

*Metlakala*

I'm Semiguul; Princess of the Strawberry. It is a name I inherit from my mother, from whom I also inherit my strengths.

At that time, my dad had a big tub in the middle of our kitchen floor, it was full of abalone, and we had to clean it, a lot of us kids. And I guess my dad saw me pouting and told me to come to the window. And he said, "See all those kids playing out there; they're not going to know how to do what we're teaching you. When you're my age, you're going to be doing this".

So true to that, I do it.

For some time now, my role has become a mother, grandmother and great-grandmother, a role that I take much pride in. As soon as my children were old enough, I would teach them all I could about our traditions. And when I say children, I mean all children of my community.

I walk through the village, I jog through the village and that's all I hear "Hi, Gram, hi Gram, hi, Gramma Fanny" and it makes me feel really good.

Every year all the families gather round, prepare their eulachons for the winter. Freezing them fresh is only one way; smoking is another. When each family has had enough, they gather their children and show them how to hang it in the smokehouse. Each family has their own unique way of hanging eulachons.

## A SAVIOUR

### Tom Robinson

*Prince Rupert*

In the early spring, in March, you get eulachon in the Nass and the Skeena - what we call... like "a saviour"- because we've struggled so hard over the winter months and that's the first fresh food that comes in and that's why the eulachon is so important to us because we've had so very little all winter and all of a sudden it's just like harvesting. You sundry it, smoke it, squeeze it for the oil. Like a medicine.

We used to pick salmonberries up at Sunnyside, Port Ed at the net-loft- it was a camp for BC Packers- and we picked up a bowl of salmonberries, we squeeze it and we add just a little bit of eulachon grease to it. That's our dessert that we just love.

*Photo: Michael Ambach*

# SALMON BURGERS

## Marty Bowles

boneless salmon fillets cut
to uniform thickness

oil

salt

lemon pepper

kaiser buns

tomatoe slices

crisp lettuce

kelp pickles (optional)

Use high smoke point oil to coat the salmon filets. Sprinkle with salt and lemon pepper, then cook over very high heat, skin side up to get grill marks, then carefully turn over the salmon and put on a cooler part of the grill until they are medium rare. Let them rest for a while after cooking.

Assemble with sauce on the bottom, then the salmon, (a couple of slices of bacon if you wish) a tomato slice or two, your favourite crisp lettuce, sauce on the top bun and serve with a few kelp pickles on the side.

## Sauce

½ C drained, plain yogurt

½ C thick sour cream

¼ C fresh dill or 1/8 C dried dill

½ jar of capers that have been chopped

zest of one lemon and the juice of half

Mix all the ingredients and chill until ready to assemble the burgers.

## SEAWEED SHINGLES

### Gary Coons

*Prince Rupert*

In Bella Bella, with my good friend William Housty, they were drying seaweed on the roofs. I'm walking down the roads in Bella Bella and I'm looking, oh, they're doing the roofs -- they're redoing the roofs and I thought they had all the shingles up there, but it's just seaweed on top of the roofs drying, and I just couldn't believe it.

And I came out of there with a sack of seaweed that somebody said, "That's worth 75 bucks!"

## IT'S STARTING TO GROW

### Fanny Nelson, Semiguul

*Metlakala*

Herring is also one of our favourites. Each year, our community members wait patiently for the herring to spawn so that we can collect its delicious eggs known to almost everyone as Roe-on-Kelp; to me xswanik (swanik) is the Sm'algyax term.

When the harvest is all done, herring has finished spawning, the cold chill is gone from the ocean. I went down to my smokehouse to assess the damage. We had a really bad winter. And I noticed (the wild rhubarb) on the ground. I thought, oh, my God, I said, "look at the beans"— it's what we call wild rhubarb —"it's starting to grow". That shows me that the seaweed is starting to grow.

Starting from the middle of May and finishing at the end of July is our seaweed season and in between seaweed the sockeye has started their run.

Sockeye season is one of the busiest seasons. Down our dock in Metlakatla, we all go down there when the fishermen come in from our community to give us our share. This is the season where you see everyone in the community down at the dock cleaning fish. Children love to come out and help their parents and learn how to clean the fish.

## SALMON ON THE GRILL

### David and Kathy Larson

*Recipe for the Freshest Wild Pacific Salmon*

1 just-caught wild [coho, chinook] salmon (any size)

salt & pepper to taste

lemon juice (2 T for each fillet)

any desired spices (dill, etc)

1 camp fire

1 sunny day

1 or more families and good friends

The salmon should be bled out and promptly filleted, taking care to keep the fillets joined at the belly.

Go light on the spices as salmon has a delicate flavour that is easily overpowered. Rub the salt, pepper and lemon juice into the flesh and place it on a wire rack in the sun until the salt starts to bring the moisture out. We use two racks out of an old refrigerator wired together for this.

When the camp fire (or grill) is down to coals (be sure it is a deep bed of coals) prop the wire racks over the coals in a shallow A-frame and drape the salmon – skin side down -over the racks. Keep the salmon 10-12 inches away from the coals.

How long it has to cook depends on how thick the fillets are. Don't be alarmed at the condition of the skin; it will be black and inedible. When the thickest flesh starts to open, take it off the fire and serve. Be sure you do not overcook it. The thicker fillets will continue to cook after they are taken off the fire so don't delay. Call in the troops and eat it hot!

Photo: Michael Ambach

### Cheese and cracker spread to use up your leftover salmon

1 C cooked salmon, bones removed

½ C cream cheese warmed to room temperature

¼ – ½ t cayenne pepper

Use a medium sized bowl. With a fork, mix and stir all the ingredients into a fine paste. Serve in a bowl on a platter surrounded with several different kinds of crackers and dry breads.

Seiner Photo: Moyna MacIlroy

## GOOD FOR THAT WINTER

### Chief Allan Wilson, Sgaann 7iw7waans (Big Killer Whale, the boss)

*Old Massett, Haida Gwaii*

We go to the Yakoun River to get sockeye. It's so vital to our gathering of food; for the sockeye, as you know, is a prized salmon.

I remember one of my friends was — we were down at the Yakoun and he was busy with the canner. I didn't know a thing about it but I helped him anyway. "Gee, it would be perfect."

But, it would cut the top off and he would lose that can. We looked at it for a long time. And we figured it out and we were able to can the salmon so he was good for that winter.

## BORROWED A PRESSURE COOKER

### Shannon Vanderheide

*Oona River*

I remember the first time my husband and I canned sockeye. We were 21 and borrowed a pressure cooker from his mom when we got the call on the VHF to come get our fish. We rode up to Moore Cove at the mouth of the Skeena, where a local fisherman was hauling his net.

I had never seen commercial gillnetting before, and it was fascinating to help haul in the glistening silver salmon. We raced back home, where we stayed up until two in the morning canning the beautiful red sockeye. I took so many pictures of the rows of jars. I was so proud of them.

## AWARD WINNING OLYMPIA SALMON MARINADE

### Debi Smith

I salmon filet,
skin on one side

I long glass pan or plastic
bag for marinating fish in

I T dark soy sauce

I T olive oil

I T freshly minced garlic

½ T fresh lemon juice

2 dashes hot sauce

The ingredient measurements are only a base; they can easily be doubled, tripled, or whatever you need according to the size of fish.

Mix the marinade. Place the salmon in a long glass cooking pan flesh side down or into the plastic bag. Pour the marinade into the pan or bag. (If the salmon is over an inch thick, slice slits on the top of the meat first so the marinade can get down into the meat). Fasten the top of the bag with a clip. Place on the counter flesh side down.

Marinate 30-60 minutes before pouring out the marinade and saving it for basting.

On a highly heated BBQ, spray the grill with non-stick spray. Place the salmon on skin side down. Turn heat down low and close the lid. After 10 minutes, open the lid and pour on the remaining reserved marinade. DO NOT FLIP the salmon at any time. Close lid and let cook another 10 minutes or until the flesh is firm to the touch (takes longer if more than one inch thick). Remove from the grill using a large flat flipper.

*Photos: Michael Ambach & Yvonne Collins*

Photo: Moyna MacIlroy

## FISH ON MY DOORSTEP

### Gary Coons

*Prince Rupert*

I taught a special class with some disadvantaged kids, and I think I learned a lot from one of my students. He was Haida, Wayne Young. I learned a lot from Wayne. You know, he fished with his dad and did food fishing-- ceremonial fishing-- and every once in a while there'd be a fish on my doorstep and we really appreciated that.

## FILL OUR BUCKETS

### Fanny Nelson, Semiguul

*Metlakala*

Our sockeye season runs from June through August, and in between we are either on the beach with our children showing them how to collect sea prunes or walking amongst the bushes and picking salmonberries, trying to fill our buckets with salmonberries.

## CANNING SALMON

### Talk around the dock

Sockeye and pinks are the main choice for canning.

Go to Bernardin's website for the basics of canning salmon.

Choose your salmon; the higher the oil content the better. Many gillnetters who fish the whole BC coast from the Fraser River to the Nass, do their canning with Skeena sockeye. Try to get ocean caught. Salmon stop eating before they enter the river and they use up their oil quickly as they swim upriver against the current, and they use it out of their fillet first!

Ocean caught pinks are an amazing high quality fish.

Northerners often half smoke their salmon before canning.

*Photo: Michael Ambach*

**Canning Halibut**

fresh halibut

small leg segments of Dungeness crab

Just follow the Bernardin salmon method; substituting halibut. But if you like crab, try this. Add a small crab leg segment into the jar with the raw halibut. When the canning process is complete, the jars have cooled, and you finally get to taste it, the result is absolutely delicious!

*Photo: Michael Ambach*

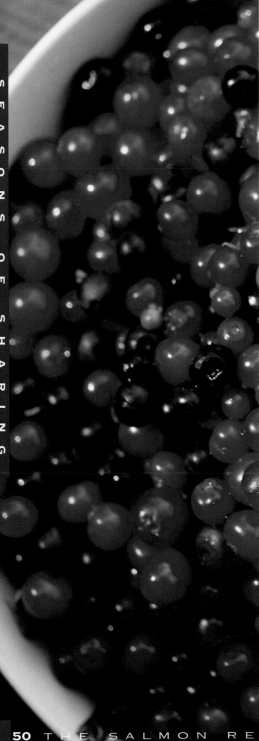

## MY OWN BERRY PICKERS!

Chris Bolten

*Hartley Bay, Gitga'at*

*Photo: Yvonne Collins*

I even have my own berry pickers. I retired from berry picking a few years ago. So my wife, Yvonne, and TJ, her good friend TJ, are the two main people that I take out and they take out their daughters or another friend.

I remember when I was leaving one day, someone just said, "Well, there goes Chris Bolton and his berry pickers".

My wife said, "Who said that?"

I teased her: "I did". I thought it sounded good: "his berry pickers".

When they're out berry picking, they go through the bushes. (They don't have trails or electronics) but you can hear them joking when they come back to the boat. "Gees, my GPS is pretty right on!" And another one of them said, "Well, mine was out just a bit". Wherever they go around there, when they pick out certain spots where I'm to pick them up, most of the time they're right on. So their GPS is up here. (Points to temple) They know the territory.

Since I retired picking berries, what I do while they're picking is I go out fishing.

## AN ARTFORM

Fanny Nelson, Semiguul

*Metlakala*

After the jars are all done, smokehouse is lit up so that we can smoke our fish. Sometimes our people have turned it into an art form. There are ways that we like to make our own by adding different kinds of flavouring.

*Photo: Michael Ambach*

Photo: Yvonne Collins

# GREEN GRILLED SALMON BELLY DINNER SALAD

## Shannon Vanderheide

*This has become a tradition for our family on the day we can sockeye each year. Inspired by both an amazing lunch at the Cow Bay Cafe and an abundance of herbs in the garden, coinciding with canning sockeye!*

mixed fresh herbs
(cilantro, basil, dill, parsley)
enough to fill a blender with

1 bulb garlic

1 t salt

olive oil

mixed salad greens

julienned carrots, cucumber,
green onion, red onion,
red/yellow/orange peppers

baby tomatoes or
chopped regular tomatoes

salmon bellies

1/3 C balsamic vinegar

2/3 C olive oil

2-4 T maple syrup
depending on your taste

This recipe serves as many as you have guests eating it. Count on 2 bellies per person as they are quite rich. Prepare the salmon bellies by removing any of the membrane or bone that may be on them, but leave the skin on as it is easier to grill them that way. You can remove it before serving if you'd like.

Mix up the first 4 ingredients in the blender, adding enough olive oil to make the green sauce of thick salad dressing consistency. Spread this on the fish and leave until you are ready to grill or bake.

In the meantime prepare the salad greens and fixings. I like to heap everything on a big platter so everyone can make up their own salad as they like it.

To make the dressing mix the balsamic vinegar, olive oil and maple syrup. Whisk with a fork until it is incorporated and adjust to your own taste. Grill the salmon skin side down on a hot barbeque until fish is done (loses its translucent colour.) Serve on top of the salad and drizzle with the dressing.

Photo: Moyna MacIlroy

# THAT'S BLACK COD!

## Chief Allan Wilson, Sgaann 7iw7waans

*Old Massett, Haida Gwaii*

One year there was a fishery in the south part of the island, they had dog salmon, and in the fall they get all -- some people call them ugly -- but they all get camouflage when they're going up the river, the dog salmon, and their teeth come out like that. They look like dogs.

But the boys had some that they opened up, took the eggs from and the dog salmon is really good for smoking and they said, "We only allow you 30." I said, "Great," he gave me 30, I started on them right away.

Later that afternoon they stopped by and they said, "Some people didn't want any, we have some more. How many do you want?" I said, "Well, whatever you can spare, I can do it for -- I can smoke some for other people." They gave me 60. So I worked on 90 that day and I smoked them over the next two days.

I don't know how many bags we had, but I brought some to my Aunt Adelia and she was so pleased. I think we gave her about 20 bags or something. And then we went to other Elders. I was so happy giving it away I forgot to keep some for myself. I think we kept about a dozen bags out of all that.

But later on Adelia's two boys took some out and they cooked it and she said, "I thought this was dog salmon. How come you's calling it dog salmon? That's black cod." And they laughed, they said "No, it's dog salmon." To me it was a real big haaw'a, a big thank you, because I prepared it properly and she enjoyed it that much.

# Barbecued Salmon with Teriyaki Marinade

## Jim Martin

1 bottle of white wine (Pinot Grigio)

1 C light soy sauce

1-2 T fresh minced ginger (jarred is OK)

2 T fresh minced garlic (jarred is OK)

4 T brown sugar

¼ cup oil (olive oil preferred)

½ can ginger ale

Combine all ingredients except wine in a large Ziploc bag. Prepare a 6-8 pound sockeye, pink or coho salmon. Fillet, remove fins, leave the skin on, and cut into chunks 3-4 in. square. Place in bag with the marinade for 1-2 hours max.

Have 1 glass wine!

Barbecue the fish skin-side down on medium-high heat until centre of fish is still red not yet pink, or if white fat starts to show on surface. Take off grill leaving burnt skin behind. Place in covered dish for 5 min. and serve with the wine.

Photo: Michael Ambach

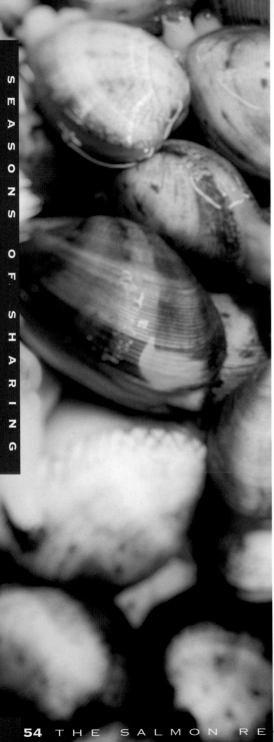

## WINTER BUTTER CLAMS

Allan Davidson, Guskin,
(Seagulls Diving for Fish)

*Old Massett, Haida Gwaii*

We would go to north beach in the winter and gather butter clams. One of the highlights of that was picking up my great-uncle Victor Adams. We'd pick him up on the way.

He would come with us, and he and my dad— they'd both sit there cleaning the clams as I dug them. I remember the joy that we got from that, sitting — the three of us sitting there, both of them speaking in Haida, laughing, having a good time.

## SANGAN RIVER MEDITATION

Susan Musgrave

*Haida Gwaii*

*Across the river, children
are eating snow, their lips
the colour of tiny kingfishers
in the numbing cold. The delight
they take in the melting of each
snowflake on their tongues reminds me:
joy is there, in everything, and even
when we can't see it.*

Photo: Ken McCormick

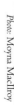

Photo: Moyna MacIlroy

## PINEAPPLE EXPRESS

### Donna McNeil Clark

*All my family likes to cook. My brother was a chef in Victoria and he taught me this recipe.*

I filleted salmon

I t minced fresh ginger

chopped chives

3 cloves minced fresh garlic

½ C brown sugar

½ T Chinese dried, salted black beans

¼ C pineapple juice

juice of ½ lime

Score the fillets. Place the fish skin side down on a flat, cooking sheet or tin foil liner. Sprinkle on the brown sugar and all the herbs and spices. Mix the juices and sprinkle over the fillets with juice in the pan around the fillets, almost to cover. Sprinkle the salted beans over the top.

Barbecue all vegetables and other foods first. Colourful skewered vegetables and pineapple chunks are oiled and mixed with lemon balm and cilantro or preferred herbs. As they are grilled they are brushed with an orange sauce or dressing. Then pre-heat the barbecue to 400 °F. Put the pan and fish on the grill. Keep the lid down for approximately ten minutes. When the skin sticks to the pan it is done.

Decorate the plate with grilled pineapple and sliced lemon or lime.

SEASONS OF SHARING

## POTLATCHES

**Reg Davidson,
Skil kaatl'aas (Spirit
Weath who is rising),
Hlk 'yaan K'ustaan
Sgaanuwee (Frog Spirit),
Kiidlajuuwee
(bow of the canoe that
cuts the water in half)**

*Haida Gwaii*

All my life, I've been a fisherman. I was taught by my dad and my grandfather. And the number one staple food for me is fish. And we live on an island where we all depend on the ocean, and our number one food that we eat, it comes from the ocean.

When we have our ceremonies, our potlatches, the food that we serve comes from the ocean. At our potlatches, I'm talking about an average of a thousand people coming here. These are the people that we serve our seafood to.

As long as I've been alive and for generations, there's been abundance of food here. To have a potlatch, we call our friends and we'll get food and we serve it to all the guests that arrive.

*Roe On Kelp Photo: Yvonne Collins*

# SCOTTISH METHOD FOR COLD SMOKED SALMON

## Thomas Spiller

*This is a recipe for smoking sockeye salmon as told by Tom who has lived in the Prince Rupert area all his life, and began smoking salmon at about the age of sixteen. He thinks spring salmon is just about as good for this smoking method but likes sockeye best as they are a perfect size and have the best storage life. His custom is to smoke after the bugs are gone (fall) or before they come out (spring). You want cool weather for a cold smoke. Use fish which has been frozen..*

3 parts pickling or rock salt

1 part brown demarara sugar

Fillet the fish, but leave the skin on.

Combine the salt and sugar to make up the salt mix. Layer the fish in your tub or container with the salt mixture below, between each layer of fish and then on top. The fish sits in the mixture for 6-8 hours. This draws juices out. After 6 hours, check by cutting a chunk, rinsing, and tasting to see if it is the right firmness. This will be close to the firmness you want at the end of the process.

Depending on the type of smoke house, you either slit the fillet to hang by the tail or put on racks skin side down. Leave it to hang at least one day before you start the smoke. You then run the smoke for about 3 days or to your own taste. Tom uses green alder with the bark off. Commercial chips can be used. Let the fish hang for another day for it to harden.

For storage it is best to vacuum pack and then freeze.

SEAFOOD ECOSYSTEM

Photo: Moyna MacIlroy

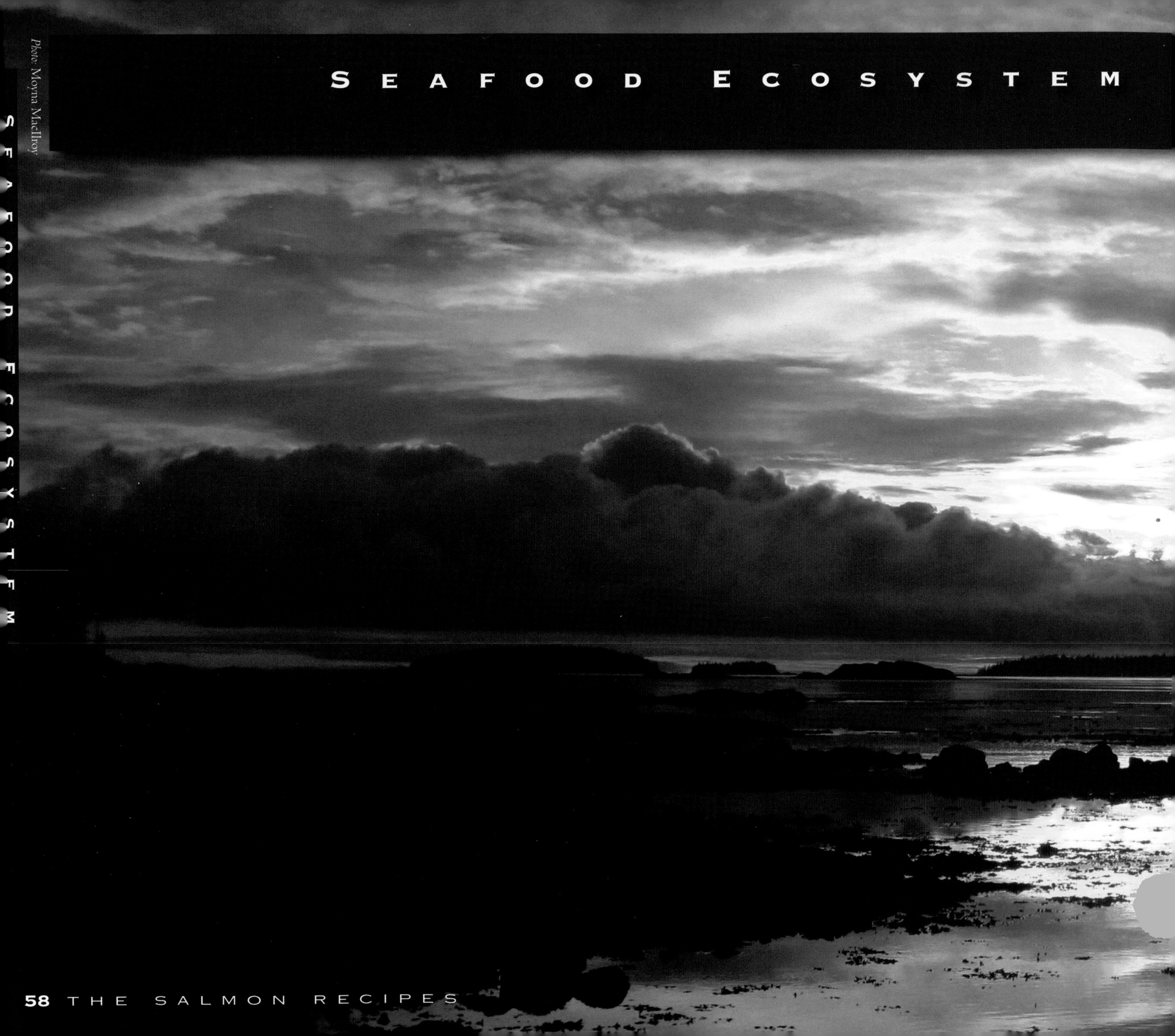

# Whitefish and Shellfish



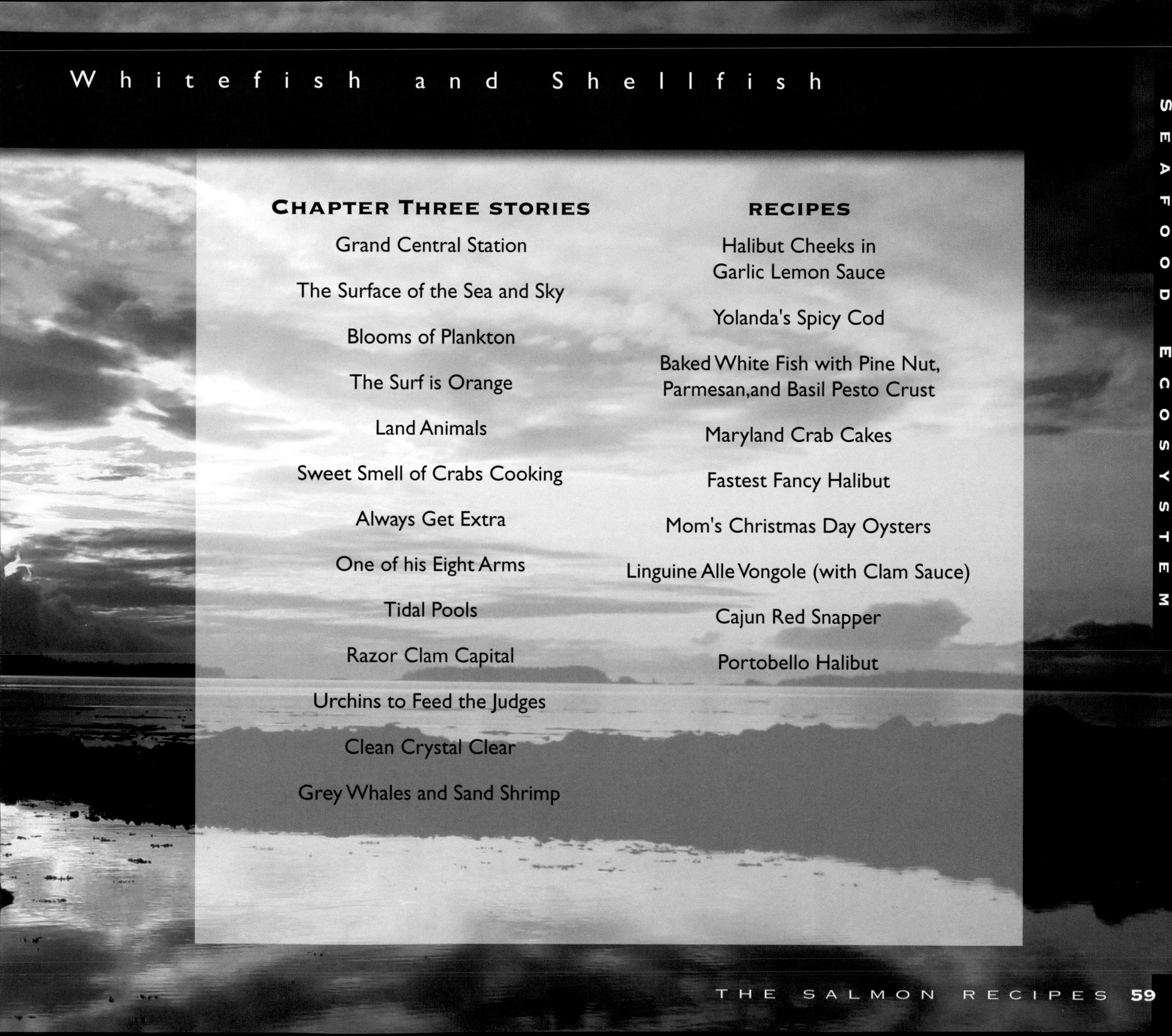

## Chapter Three Stories

Grand Central Station

The Surface of the Sea and Sky

Blooms of Plankton

The Surf is Orange

Land Animals

Sweet Smell of Crabs Cooking

Always Get Extra

One of his Eight Arms

Tidal Pools

Razor Clam Capital

Urchins to Feed the Judges

Clean Crystal Clear

Grey Whales and Sand Shrimp

## Recipes

Halibut Cheeks in Garlic Lemon Sauce

Yolanda's Spicy Cod

Baked White Fish with Pine Nut, Parmesan,and Basil Pesto Crust

Maryland Crab Cakes

Fastest Fancy Halibut

Mom's Christmas Day Oysters

Linguine Alle Vongole (with Clam Sauce)

Cajun Red Snapper

Portobello Halibut

Photo: Moyna MacIlroy

## GRAND CENTRAL STATION

### Glenn Naylor

*Prince Rupert*

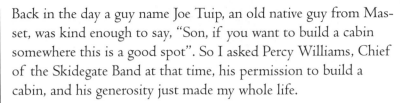

Back in the day a guy name Joe Tuip, an old native guy from Masset, was kind enough to say, "Son, if you want to build a cabin somewhere this is a good spot". So I asked Percy Williams, Chief of the Skidegate Band at that time, his permission to build a cabin, and his generosity just made my whole life.

So I built a cabin down there and we lived off the land for a couple of winters and we hiked and canoed up and down the coast and found Burnaby Narrows. The story was that if you had no arms or legs and were deaf, dumb and blind, you could roll down the beach and eat in Burnaby Narrows.

There's more protein per square foot on that little patch of ground than anywhere in the world. It is amazing. It's like Grand Central Station when the tide is down. I mean, there's stuff going off everywhere.

## THE SURFACE OF THE SEA AND SKY

### Luanne Roth

*Prince Rupert*

The surface of the sea and the sky might be grey but the red orange cloud on the sounder means tons of needlefish. The kind of needlefish which burst out still almost live from a just caught chinook in the cleaning trough.

# HALIBUT CHEEKS IN GARLIC LEMON SAUCE

## Karen Stepko

*Shannon Vanderheide cooked this for our photo*

2 T butter

1 large red onion, chopped

5 cloves garlic, sliced

1 T salt

1 T chopped chives

zest from 2 lemons

juice from ½ lemon

½ cup white wine

2 T capers

1 lb halibut (or lingcod) cheeks

Melt the butter over medium-high heat, then add onion and garlic and sauté until translucent. Add the salt, chives, lemon zest and juice, and the wine, and reduce by 1/3. Add capers and stir. Then add the halibut cheeks and cook 3-4 min. on each side.

SEAFOOD ECOSYSTEM

## BLOOMS OF PLANKTON

### Des Nobels

*Dodge Cove*

Through my experience in fishing this area, gillnetting and longlining, I've noticed a range of interesting events. After a good rain, what will happen— depending on sunlight and temperature— the nutrients create huge blooms of phytoplankton and zooplankton which attract an immense array of marine fish. Without that, there is no food base. That cycle ensures that we continue to see the broader marine environment.

I've seen some incredible sights when fishing there over the years.. Large schools of juvenile sable fish (black cod, as most people know it) which is always considered a deepwater fish, but as juveniles they live in these inside waters where it's protected, where there's a large food resource base and protection from larger marine predators.

Within that mass and body of bloom are larval stages of many different types of fish, invertebrates and crustaceans. Larval crabs have covered my net as a bloom takes place. The larva feed on the plankton, then drift out through the tides into the outer marine areas and settle on the bottom, providing us and other marine mammals with food.

 The deep channels here are home to some very interesting creatures. When longlining for halibut we have seen Pacific sleeper sharks and sixgill sharks in the depths. It is my understanding that these are all juveniles. They're there for the protection and for the food that is offered to them.

# YOLANDA'S SPICY COD

## Yolanda Malcolm

2 lbs. fresh Canadian cod
1 lime
3 T olive oil
small onion
1 piece of ginger
1 jalapeno pepper
2 T butter
fresh cilantro

Cut the cod in 4 oz pieces; season with lime juice and salt and pepper to taste.

Thinly slice the onion. Mince the ginger and chop the jalapeno, adding all of these with olive oil heated in a frying pan. Sauté till the onion is translucent. Add the fish and cook first on one side then the other. Add a bit of butter to brown just before serving. The total cooking time is about 7 minutes.

When serving, put all of the sauté ingredients on top of the cod and garnish with 1/2 cup. chopped cilantro.

This is a good mixture for tacos and tortillas. It is fast and not fussy. I use cod because 3 oz of Pacific cod (cooked with dry heat) equals 89 calories, 23 gm protein, and less than 1 gm fat and this recipe has no breadcrumbs etc. so it is low calorie and healthy.

SEAFOOD ECOSYSTEM

S E A F O O D   E C O S Y S T E M

## THE SURF IS ORANGE

### Ron Brown Jr.

*Old Massett, Haida Gwaii*

The Tow Hill area, it's the biggest rearing area for the Dungeness crab, the razor clam, the scallops, cod eggs, rock scallops, mussels, and there's also a big habitat area for shark. You can always see the shark packages washed up on shore, and the halibut all over in June and July on all the beaches, right on the sand; you could see the little guys.

But when you see the crab and the clams start to spawn, you'd be amazed at the colour the water turns. As far as you can see, the whole surf is orange and brown. As I say, we do not want to put any of this at risk. As the fishermen explained, the waters go north and south. So the oil would be carried from the mainland to here. Then it would go west and it would cover every part of our beaches.

## LAND ANIMALS

### Dora Moody, Mantxa'apsgan, (Woman on Four Poles)

*Kitkatla, Gitxaala*

About the deer going down to eat kelp off the beach. You know, there are lots of different mammals — land mammals that do that and that. So it would not only affect the sea, but it would affect the land animals as well.

## BAKED WHITE FISH WITH PINE NUT, PARMESAN, AND BASIL PESTO CRUST

This recipe is used with permission from kalynskitchen.com and she mentions it was adapted from Cooking New American.

*Jianping likes this recipe very much.*

2 white fish fillets, about 6 oz. each (halibut, lingcod, or rockfish)

3 T pine nuts

2 T Parmesan cheese

1/4 t finely minced garlic (I garlic clove)

I t basil pesto (I used purchased pesto)

I 1/2 T mayo (use regular or light mayo, not fat-free)

This makes 2 servings, but the recipe can be doubled or tripled.

Preheat oven or toaster oven to 400° F. Spray individual casserole dishes with non-stick spray or olive oil (or use one large casserole dish if you don't have individual ones). Remove the fish fillets from the refrigerator and let them come to room temperature while the oven heats. (Having the fish at room temperature is very important or it won't cook before the crust topping gets too brown).

Use a large chef's knife to finely chop the pine nuts and mince the garlic. Mix together chopped pine nuts, Parmesan cheese, minced garlic, basil pesto, and mayo.

Use a rubber scraper to spread the crust mixture evenly over the surface of each fish fillet. Pile it on so all the crust mixture is used. Bake fish 10-15 minutes, until fish is firm to the touch and crust mixture is starting to lightly brown. Serve hot.

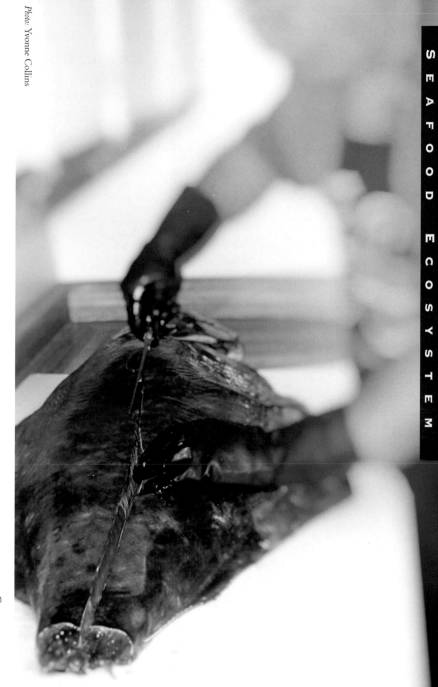

*Photo: Yvonne Collins*

## SWEET SMELL OF CRABS COOKING

### Cameron Hill, Aayawk, Ha'gwil laxhaand, and Ka'gwaays

*Hartley Bay Gitga'at Nation*

There's nothing that makes me feel better than to have my crab cooking outside of my father's house or my house and to have people walk by and smell it… and …to share what I have.

Photo: Yvonne Collins

Photo: Yvonne Collins

# MARYLAND CRAB CAKES

## Lou Allison

2 slices bread,
crusts removed

1 T mayonnaise

1 T Worcestershire sauce

1 T parsley flakes or 2 T
minced fresh parsley

1 T baking powder

1 t Old Bay seasoning
(I use more to taste, never
had a complaint)

¼ t salt

1 egg, beaten

1 lb crab meat, give or take

*I learned about these crab cakes from my spouse Jeremiah's children in Maryland, a state that is famous for both crab cakes and fried chicken. The secret ingredient is the Old Bay seasoning, a 60-year-old spice mix originating in the Chesapeake Bay area. This recipe is from the side of the iconic Old Bay can, with a few small changes. The local Dungeness crab meat is excellent in this. (Old Bay seasoning is available locally at Maverick Mart in Prince Rupert.).*

Break bread into small pieces and moisten with milk. Add remaining ingredients and shape lightly into cakes. Fry in hot olive oil until golden brown

Photo: Michael Ambach

## ALWAYS GET EXTRA

Chief Allan Wilson,
Sgann 7iw7waans
(Big Killer Whale, the boss)

*Old Massett*

What we really go after are the razor clams. We get them for canning. We get them for freezing so we can have fresh chowder.

We go along the North Beach to get butter clams. A lot of our young men go out to the North Beach just behind our village here to dig clams in the fall. And a lot of them always get extra, too, which is really nice.

## ONE OF HIS EIGHT ARMS

Luanne Roth

*Prince Rupert*

Once in our prawn trap there was a small octopus holding a prawn. He was a bit scared and disoriented, but the whole time we had him out of the water, tipping the trap to have a better look as he pulled himself around, he kept one of his eight arms outstretched with the end carefully holding his prawn.

Photo: Moyna MacIlroy

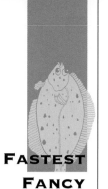

# FASTEST FANCY HALIBUT

## Debi Smith

lingcod or halibut cut into 1" thick slabs of individual serving pieces

fine, dry breadcrumbs

equal parts of powdered and real Parmesan cheese

dash of salt and pepper

olive oil

Heat oven to 425° F. Dip the fish pieces in olive oil, coating all sides before rolling in the breadcrumbs and cheese. Place on a tinfoil lined baking sheet or in a glass pan.

Cook for 10 minutes or until fish is no longer translucent inside.

Serve with tartar sauce.

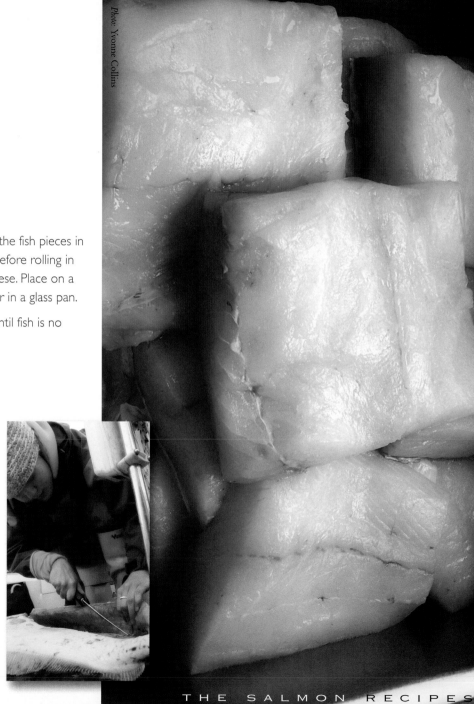

Photo: Yvonne Collins

Photo: Mae Jong-Bowles

*Photo: Michael Ambach*

## TIDAL POOLS

### Oliver Bell, Gliii glaa, which means Calm Sea.

*Old Massett, Haida Gwaii*

Now, I do charters for salmon, halibut, cod, crab, and sightseeing.

In 1984, I had taken a little break from seining and worked for another outfit and started a family. I worked for BC Parks branch on the East Coast of Naikoon Park.

Due to weather, a large barge with 130 tons of diesel and 30 tons of gasoline was wrecked on the beaches in front of Eagle Creek. I had the opportunity to work with a surveyor to assess the damage and what I saw was devastating.

On the rocks, there were no barnacles, kelp or seaweed and under the rocks, there were no crabs, no life of any kind in the tidal pools. In the tidal pools, normally you would find little bullheads, eels, flounders, snails.

*Editors Note: The tankers Enbridge is proposing would carry about one thousand times more oil than this "large" barge carried.*

## RAZOR CLAM CAPITAL

### Richard Russ Jones, Nang Jingwas

*Haida Gwaii*

From talking to people from Cordova, 20 years after Exxon Valdez, you know, they've lost their Dungeness crab fishery in that area and they used to have a big Dungeness crab fishery and this is more than 20 years, you know, after — after the oil spill.

Cordova used to be called the Razor Clam Capital in Alaska because they had beaches similar to what we have here and they had a large razor clam fishery. There's currently no razor clam fishery there. Basically the clams, you know, haven't come back in that area.

Photo: Michael Ambach

# Mom's Christmas Day Oysters

## N. Carol Brown

*This is a custom I started with my kids on Christmas because I'll always remember when I was a single mom on income assistance. I was living on Cortez Island with my three year old daughter at the time and in the channel was the most beautiful bed of silver white oysters that provided me with fresh marine protein during the winter. To this day, I love fresh pan-fried oysters.*

fresh ground coffee

fresh BC oysters

I fresh farm egg

2 T olive oil

2 T butter

I cup whole wheat flour

powdered kelp or
ground kelp (or salt)

½ cup of half and half cream

I lime

Enjoy your coffee or Brown Cow as the cast iron frying pan or grill is heating up to medium heat. Rinse the oysters and lay them on a paper towel. Mix the egg in a bowl and have the flour leveled on a plate, add kelp for salt. Put the oysters in the egg, coat them, remove and roll them in the flour. Add at least two T of oil to the grill and add the butter after the oil is heated through. Add the oysters quickly after the butter. Cook on one side till golden brown, turn. It may take only 3-4 minutes.

They take 7-10 minutes depending on the size of oyster. An overcooked oyster has less flavour. It is advised that the core temperature of the oysters be 70 degrees C. or 160 degrees F. At this point either put them on a serving plate and into a warm oven or place them on prepared plates. Brown a tsp. of flour then pour ¼ cup of cream into the pan. The sauce should bubble. Add as much cream again. Scrape the good flavour of the pan as you stir until sauce thickens. Pour the sauce over your oysters.

They can be served with a slice of lime and toasted Baguette and a light brunch fruit salad.

## URCHINS TO FEED THE JUDGES

### Warren Nelson, Ama gydem naat

*Kitkatla, Gitxaala*

Me and two of my brothers went out that morning at low water to go get ts'akwe'ats (urchins) through the pass over here to feed everybody at lunch.

(The Canadian National Energy Board panel of judges held a hearing in Kitkakla to help evaluate Enbridge's oil tanker proposal. Their lunch was supplied by the village)

*Photo: Moyna MacIlroy*

SEAFOOD ECOSYSTEM

# Linguine Alle Vongole (with clam sauce)

### Karen Fait

1 lb linguine

6 lbs fresh clams or 12 oz canned clams & clam liquid

2 C cold water

¼ C dry white wine

1 small onion, diced

1 bay leaf

6 T butter

1½ t garlic, finely chopped

3 T fresh parsley, finely chopped

1/3 C dry white wine

salt & pepper

Cook the fresh pasta al dente, 3-5 minutes; 5-7 minutes for packaged linguine.

If you are using fresh clams, wash them with cold running water to remove sand, then put them in a pot. Add water, wine, onion and bay leaf to pot, cover and bring to a boil on high heat. Steam the clams for 7-10 minutes until their shells open. Some clams will not open – discard these. Drain pot, re-serving ½ C liquid. Remove clams from shells.

Sauté garlic in butter in a large skillet on medium heat. Add the clams, clam liquid and parsley to garlic, stir until well blended and reduce by simmering on medium heat for 4 minutes. Add the wine to the garlic mixture and reduce by simmering on medium heat for 2 more minutes. Salt and pepper to taste.

Add linguine to garlic mixture and toss and heat. Put linguine into a warm serving bowl or on warm plates and serve. Serves 4-6 people.

Photo: Michael Ambach

Photo: Michael Ambach

## CLEAN CRYSTAL CLEAR

### Glenn Naylor

*Prince Rupert*

From traveling around the world I don't think there are very many places left that are as clean as this one. This place is really, really clean. If you go out on the water and hang out there, you might find some flotsam and jetsam, but the water is always clean, crystal clear, gorgeous. Except when there's a bloom and then it gets a bit thick. There are high-level reefs around too, that support lots of life.

Photo: Moyna MacIlroy

# Cajun Red Snapper

## N. C. Brown

I ½ lbs red snapper

½ C pecans, finely chopped

½ C corn flour
or corn meal if preferred

½ t salt or crushed
dried kelp

½ t fresh ground
black pepper

3/4 t cayenne pepper

2 T maple syrup

olive oil

Wash the fillets. Place on paper towel to dry. Mix together the next five ingredients on a flat plate. Using a pastry brush, coat one side of the fillets with maple syrup. Place syrup side down on nut and flour mixture.

Brush the other side. Turn to coat the second side. Do the same with all the fillets while the frying pan is heating to medium. Add at least 2 T of oil. When pan is hot, lay the fillets into the pan. Fry at least 4 minutes on each side. May add butter for added flavour near end of cooking time. There should be some blackened crust before removing from heat. Serves 4.

Photo: Michael Ambach

*Photo: Moyna MacIlroy*

# GREY WHALES AND SAND SHRIMP

## Elvis Davis, NaayKun K'iigawaay Clan

*Old Masset, Haida Gwaii*

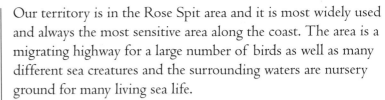

Our territory is in the Rose Spit area and it is most widely used and always the most sensitive area along the coast. The area is a migrating highway for a large number of birds as well as many different sea creatures and the surrounding waters are nursery ground for many living sea life.

In August and September, the grey whales migrate along the coast and feed on sand krill — sand shrimps. And they go right up to the beach up to twenty feet away, which I've witnessed quite a few times because I like to be in that area watching lots of different mammals and animals that migrate through there.

*Humpback Whale Photo:* Doug Davies

*Photo: Michael Ambach*

## PORTOBELLO HALIBUT

### Doug Laird

3½ T extra-virgin olive oil

2 medium shallots, finely chopped

½ lb. portobello (or shiitake) mushrooms, stemmed and sliced ¼ inch thick

¼ C heavy cream

1 t chopped fresh thyme

kosher salt and freshly ground black pepper

2 C lightly packed baby spinach leaves

4 6-oz boneless, skin-on (or not) fillets

3 T fresh lemon juice

toasted pinenuts

Heat 2 T of the oil in a 12-inch nonstick skillet over medium-high heat. Add the shallots and cook, stirring often, until golden brown, about 2 minutes. Add the mushrooms and cook, stirring occasionally, until softened, 3 to 4 minutes. Stir in the cream, thyme, lots of salt, and 1/8 t pepper. Reduce the heat to medium and cook, stirring often, until thickened, 1 to 2 minutes. Remove the skillet from the heat and stir in the spinach until wilted. Transfer to a bowl and cover with foil to keep warm. Clean the skillet and return it to the stove.

Heat the remaining 1½ T oil in the skillet over medium heat. Season the halibut fillets all over with lots of salt and pepper. Arrange the halibut in the skillet skin side up in a single layer and cook, turning once, until golden brown and just cooked through, 7 to 9 minutes total. Plate the halibut on the warm mushroom/spinach mixture.

Mix the lemon juice with 1 tbsp water, add to the skillet, and cook, scraping up any browned bits, until just thickened, about 30 seconds. Drizzle the pan juices over the halibut. Sprinkle with pine nuts. They can be toasted prior in a dry hot pan.

Photo: Michael Ambach

WILD WINDS

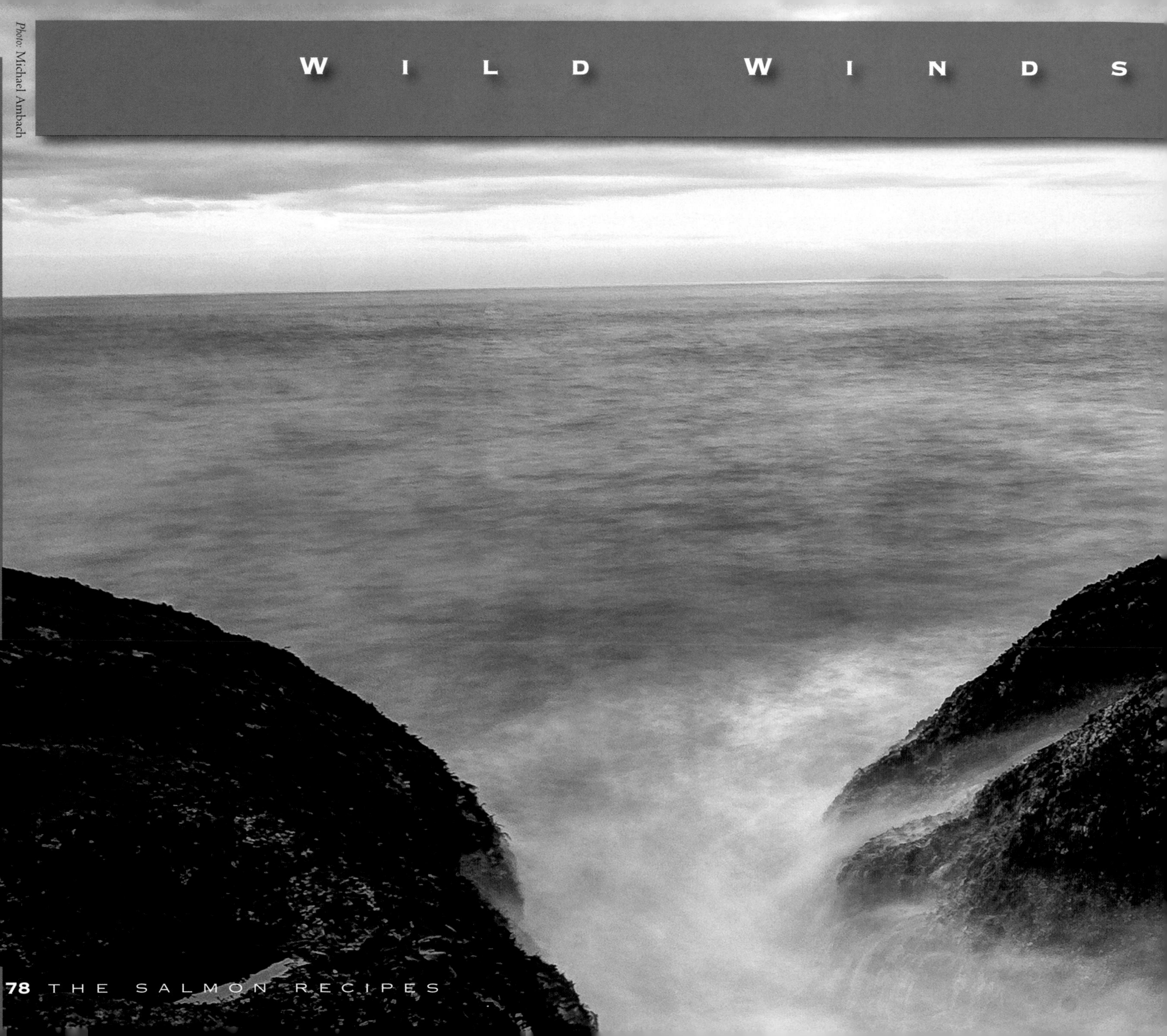

## QUEEN OF THE NORTH SINKING

### Daniel Danes, Skiigoxt ahow

*Hartley Bay, Gitga'at*

The Queen of the North sank in 2006 and my friend and I were the first ones out there. I was running a hatchery boat. We picked those people up.

When we got there, he hollered for his niece, "Leanne, where are you?" And she shook the rubber raft and said, "I'm right here." Then I said, "Who's in charge here?" And the guy on the fibreglass lifeboat flashed his light and he said, "I am." And I said, "I think you better take these kids and these old people into Hartley Bay right now because they're getting prepared for you."

And I took eight people on, four adults and four kids on my speedboat. It was a 19-foot boat. It had a 90 horse on it. It went pretty good. It was dark and on the way in, I was reading the mountains and the fellow who was on with me was flashing the light so I wouldn't hit any logs.

Just when we were coming in the pass, the people I had on from the ferry said, "Look, she's going down." I turned around and that's when we saw the ferry just go down like that!

## ONE LITTLE MISTAKE

### Sarah Burgess

*Prince Rupert*

Look at the Queen of the North; that ship had done that route hundreds, thousands of times. If you calculate how many times they made that trip, that track record looks pretty darn good, but it only took one little mistake and now that ship is at the bottom of the ocean.

# AWARD WINNING SMOKED SALMON CHOWDER

## Shiney O'Neil

One 4"x 4" piece of smoked salmon (skin as well) or one ½ pint smoked salmon canned

5 C water

4 large cloves of garlic

dash of Worcestershire

¼ t thyme (rub crushed)

½ C onions

½ C celery

1 C diced potatoes (peeled or with skin)

2 t chopped chives (optional)

1 vegetable/chicken stock cube (optional)

pinch of black pepper

1 package (250 g) cream cheese

1 C of any kind of milk

1 t lemon or lime juice

Splash of white wine (optional)

3 or 4 T white flour or other thickening agent

Place salmon, garlic, Worcestershire and thyme into pan with the 5 cups of water, bring to a boil then turn to medium heat. Cut up the onion, celery and potatoes, keeping the potatoes separate. Simmer the salmon for 15 to 20 minutes, remove the garlic and put through garlic press or just mash up and put back into pot with salmon. Taste the stock and add the stock cube if needed for flavor and salt content, add pepper. Add the onion and celery and cook for 10 minutes. Remove the salmon, cut it up and then put it back in. Add the potatoes and chives.

While this is simmering, place milk, cheese, wine and half the lemon or lime juice into blender and blend. Add the flour and blend again. Check that the potatoes are cooked and turn the heat up slightly — pour in the blended mix and stir well.

Reduce heat to medium low, taste for salt and flavour and add salt if required and the rest of the lemon or lime juice. Simmer to thicken and the chowder is ready to serve with hearty bread.

Photo: Michael Ambach

WILD WINDS

## HEAVY OVERFALLS AND TIDE RIPS

### Oliver Bell, Gliii glaa (Calm Sea)

*Haida Gwaii, Old Massett*

Rose Spit and Learmonth Bank are two of the most dangerous areas. Rose Spit is a sandbar that reaches into the Hecate Straits which creates a lot of turbulence. Traveling through this area can be terrifying in big tides. Where the shallow water meets the deep water strong tiderips and heavy overfalls occur.

Learmonth Bank is a shallow area north of Langara Island which can cause huge swells after a westerly storm, creating dangerous overfalls and rips again. Learmonth Bank is kind of halfway between here and Alaska -- Langara and Alaska -- and that's where the shipping lane is.

## DIVING SIMPSON ROCK

### Luanne Roth

*Prince Rupert*

*Our region has exceptionally high tides. At peak tides, during a six hour period, twenty feet of water from the whole of Hecate Straits moves, much of it past Rose Spit.*

A bunch of Rupert divers wanted to go see lingcod egg masses so we took them out to a breaking rock where several currents intersect. The flow and upwelling make for a spot rich with rockfish, lingcod and anemones. It is near the area where international vessels wait for pilots to board.

We picked the day to be at the month's lowest tides and the hour to be at slack and the divers were rewarded with sightings of "huge lingcod" and egg masses as 'big as watermelons". As the last diver swam the short distance back to our anchored boat the tide was starting, and swim as she might with her huge flippers she was barely making headway and tiring quickly.

With a well thrown life ring attached to a line we happily pulled her in and then stood back as she, exhausted and bewildered, angrily wondered why we had driven away from her like that.

## SWEET GINGER BROILED SALMON

### Jianping Roth

finely chopped ginger root

minced garlic

ABC soy sauce
(very sweet soy-syrup)

olive oil

salmon fillet

Cook the ginger, soya sauce and olive oil in a sauce pan over medium heat for about 2 minutes and then pour the sauce over the salmon filet. Let the salmon sit in the fridge for about 30 minutes and then broil at 400° F for about 20 minutes.

If your broiler doesn't have a temperature control it will broil at 500 ° F which is too hot. In that case you will have to check it often, turn the broiler on and off and possibly adjust the height. The flavour as a result of the broiler caramelizing the sauce is worth the trouble.

*Photo: Yvonne Collins*

*Photo: Michael Ambach*

WILD WINDS

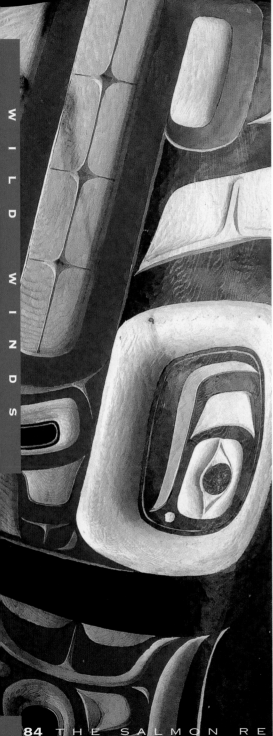

Photo: Eric Yates  Master Carver: Henry Green, Tsimshian Nation

# SOUTHEAST WIND AND HE WHO TAKES THE TOPS OFF TREES

### Robert Davidson, Guud sans glans (Eagle of the Dawn)

*Old Massett*

One of the supernatural beings that is most common among the Haida is the southeast wind or Xiiw. He is so prominent and powerful that he has ten brothers. These ten brothers are certain kinds of winds and clouds that accompany winds and tidal waves.

Some of the names of the brothers are:

*He who takes off the tops of the trees,*

*He who rattles the stones,*

*Passing away quickly,*

*He that takes away the surface of the sea,*

*He who comes before his master and melts the ice,*

*Mist,*

*He who takes off the tips of branches,*

*Canoe breaker,*

*and*

*He who blows the tops off whitecaps.*

Ten is a number that indicates social cultural completeness in Haida culture. Having ten brothers shows how important Xiiw was and how much he dominated the lives of the Haida people.

The southeast wind is the most powerful wind affecting Haida Gwaii and affects our lives deeply. He and his brothers blow up over the sea and land around Haida Gwaii, especially in the Hecate Strait and Masset Inlet.

I was crossing Hecate Strait once in a storm, in a southeast wind storm, and I counted four brothers in that storm, so not just one brother shows up at a time.

Southeast wind lives in the ocean and when he is illustrated he is shown in the form of a killer whale.

Photo: Michael Ambach

# Quinoa and Black Bean Salad

## Annie Thompson

*This salad goes nicely with salmon.*

1 T olive oil
1 t paprika
1 C raw quinoa
2 C water
1 t salt
2 T olive oil
2 C or 1 large onion, finely chopped
2-4 cloves garlic
1 t cumin & 1 t coriander
2 C corn
1 red pepper, diced
1 orange pepper, diced
1-2 t garlic chili paste or 1 fresh chili, finely chopped
1-2 T cilantro, chopped
1 C black beans, cooked
1 large tomato, diced
2 T parsley, chopped
¼ C fresh lemon juice
salt and pepper to taste

Rinse quinoa and set aside. Heat oil in saucepan over medium heat, add paprika and stir constantly for about 1 minute. Add the quinoa, water and salt. Cover and bring to a boil. Lower heat and simmer for 10-15 minutes or until the water is absorbed and quinoa is tender but still a little chewy.

In a skillet, heat oil and sauté onions, garlic, cumin and coriander until onions are translucent. Stir in corn, red peppers, chili paste and cilantro. Sauté for another 5 minutes or so.

In a large bowl, combine quinoa and sautéed veggies and chill for 15 minutes. Add black beans, tomatoes, parsley, lemon juice, salt and pepper.

_Photo: Michael Ambach_

## SIX EAGLE SKELETONS

Glenn Naylor

_Prince Rupert_

I found I think six eagle skeletons in the creek and I took a look to try and figure out who'd kill these eagles and then I realized that the southeast had killed them. The southeast had blown long enough and hard enough that they died of exposure; they couldn't fly. And it sort of gives you an idea of how brutal the North Coast actually is.

_Photo: Moyna MacIlroy_

## ROGUE WAVE

Henry Clifton,
Gnulx Hyitk

_Hartley Bay,
Gitga'at First Nation_

On a more serious subject, I was out fishing last year in May -- halibut fishing -- and we almost had an accident; I had to turn the boat fast. I'd seen a shadow coming up beside me so I looked and it just made the hair stand up on the back of my head. So I had to push the throttle, turn the boat. And I put my son in danger, because he was putting hooks on the line, setting halibut gear. But he was wondering "why did he turn?", so he turns to look and he looked up; twenty, thirty feet in the air is a wave coming. It's a rogue wave.

If I hadn't turned the boat, I wouldn't be here talking to you now. That's how fast the waves and the weather come up when we're out in Hecate Strait.

Photo: Michael Ambach

## PAN SEARED HONEY GLAZED SALMON WITH BROWNED BUTTER LIME SAUCE

Annie Thompson

4 (6 oz) salmon fillets, rested at room temperature 20 minutes

8 t flour

2 T honey

zest of 1 - 2 limes (optional)

2 T extra virgin olive oil

Prepare the browned butter lime sauce

Remove the skin from the salmon fillets if you haven't already. It's best to cook this salmon in either two batches or in two cast iron pans at once. You don't want to over-crowd the pan. Heat your cast iron pan over medium heat until hot. Drizzle the pan with 1 tbsp of olive oil and swirl to coat evenly.

Sprinkle a little flour on one side of the salmon and use your fingers to evenly coat it. Place the salmon flour side down in the hot oiled pan and coat the top with an-other sprinkle of flour. Drizzle the top with about 3/4 t of honey. Cook for about 3-5 minutes and flip over. Drizzle a bit more honey on the first side and cook for an-other 3-5 minutes or almost cooked. Flip one more time for about a minute and then plate the salmon. Remember, it's bet-ter to slightly undercook fish than to over-cook it.

Serve immediately with browned butter lime sauce drizzled over top and sprinkled with lime zest.

## Sauce

6 T salted butter, cubed
3 T fresh lime juice
1 clove garlic, minced
½ t salt
½ t freshly ground black pepper

Melt butter in a small and preferably light coloured saucepan over medium heat. Swirl the saucepan occasionally on the stove element in-stead of stirring. The butter will begin to foam and crackle. That's a great sign; that means that the water is evaporating from the butter. Once the crackling subsides, keep an eye on the butter. The butter solids will begin to brown. As it browns, it will smell very nutty. Once well browned, immediately remove the butter from the heat and place in a small bowl. Removing the butter from the pan will ensure that it doesn't continue to cook and burn in the hot pan.

Stir in the lime juice, garlic, salt and pepper. Set aside and gently stir or whisk before drizzling it over the salmon.

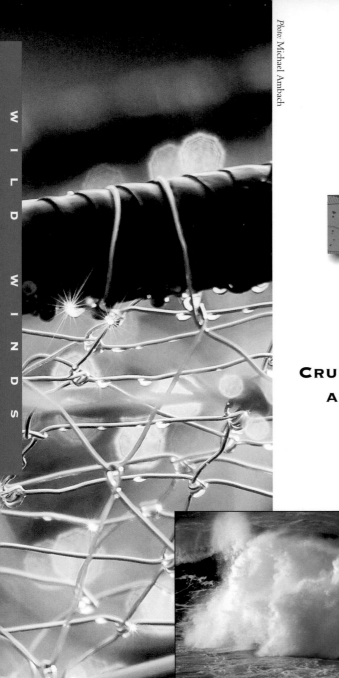

## MAYDAY

### Ian Dobson

*Prince Rupert*

Earlier this year, I worked on the Cosco Yokohama, a modern 80,000 ton container ship, with state of the art navigation and communication equipment, which lost 29 containers 100 miles off Prince Rupert. I talked to various crew members. One 30-year officer said he had never had an experience like it. A mayday was transmitted. The ship was heeling over past 35 degrees which was as far as their instrument measured. The chief engineer said it was the worst 8 or 9 hours of his life. A one ton motor was bouncing around the engine room like a ping-pong ball. Huge spare pistons which had been fitted and bolted in at the shipyards were coming loose.

## CRUNCHED LIKE A PAPER CUP

### Arnie Nagy

*Prince Rupert*

I've seen the last container ship that came in that was hit by the storm out there in Hecate Strait. And to see containers torn apart like a paper cup crunched like that scared me. I am not a man that scares easy. I am not a man that gets intimidated easily, and I was both, because everything that I'd been taught and raised and represented for all these years in the fishing industry came back to me in one massive wave of information to my brain. And that really signified to me the potential risks that I may face, that we may face, and that my industry may face should an accident occur out there on the waters with the tankers.

Photo: Renata

# POTATO SALAD WITH SMOKED SALMON

2 lbs new red potatoes, cut bite size

½ lb. smoked salmon

½ C sour cream

½ -1 t horseradish

1 t lemon juice

½ t red wine vinegar

2 t fresh dill, finely chopped

salt and pepper

capers (optional)

Boil potatoes just until tender, drain and keep warm.

Stir the dill, horseradish, vinegar and lemon juice into the sour cream. Mix the dressing into the warm potatoes and add salt and pepper to taste.

Garnish with thinly sliced smoked salmon shavings and a few capers.

Serve warm.

WILD WINDS

## OLD NORWEGIAN SALT

### Glenn Naylor

*Prince Rupert*

I'm also a stevedore, that's mostly what I do now -- the Cosco Yokohama came in under severe duress. It had had its ass kicked in so hard, it got hit -- the crew was pretty much saying it was a 100-foot wave, the crew said she was over 40 degrees, the writing in the book says 35. I don't know how many hatches had to get repaired on that vessel, but the cans that we took off were completely mangled.

So there was an old Norwegian salt on the boat that had been hired by the shipping company to come and do some of the boat inspection and I managed to get a couple of minutes to talk to him. I just asked him, I said, "You know, what do you think went on here?"

And he said, "Well, what happens out in the Pacific, you'll get a couple of different storm systems happening going at different angles and when the waves run into each other, they correspondingly increase in size. So you'll have these areas where instead of the waves being 30 or 40 feet high, they'll double or triple from the inner section of the storms."

Anyway, the crew was praying for their lives, I mean it was -- it was nasty out there. And this was two weeks ago.

## SALMON FAJITAS

### Annie Thompson

1 T olive oil

2 T fresh lime juice

2 cloves garlic, minced

1 t garlic chili paste

½ t cumin

¼ t salt

¼ t fresh ground
black pepper

1 lb salmon fillets, boneless
and skinless, sliced into
½ inch strips

2 T olive oil

1 red pepper, thinly sliced

1 yellow or orange pepper,
thinly sliced

1 small white or red onion,
thinly sliced

1 jalapeno, seeded and diced

1 T fresh lime juice

warm tortillas

optional toppings:
guacamole, salsa, cheese,
sour cream, lime wedges

In a large bowl or ziplock bag, combine marinade ingredients: oil, lime juice, garlic, chili paste, cumin, salt and pepper. Add the salmon, and toss in the marinade until evenly coated. Cover or seal and refrigerate for at least 30 minutes, or up to 5 hours.

Heat 1 T olive oil in a large skillet over medium-high heat. Add peppers, onion and jalapeno and sauté, stirring occasionally, until the onions are soft and the vegetables all begin to slightly brown on the edges. Add the lime juice and sauté for an additional minute, then plate and set aside.

Add the second T of olive oil to the skillet and gently add the salmon slices and marinade. Gently because some types of salmon are softer than others and you don't want it to fall apart. Sauté for a few minutes, flipping the salmon over to ensure it cooks evenly. When the edges begin to look slightly crispy and browned, remove from heat.

Assemble the fajitas by layering warm tortillas with the salmon, vegetable mixture and desired toppings.

Photo Michael Ambach

Photo: Moyna MacIlroy

## SEA SMOKE AND BLOWN FUSES

### Rick Haugan

*Prince Rupert*

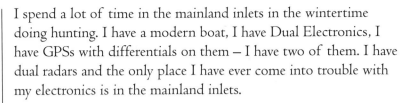

I spend a lot of time in the mainland inlets in the wintertime doing hunting. I have a modern boat, I have Dual Electronics, I have GPSs with differentials on them – I have two of them. I have dual radars and the only place I have ever come into trouble with my electronics is in the mainland inlets.

I've encountered winds over a 100 miles-an-hour that take all your aerials out of your rigging so you lose your ability to talk. The scanners on the radars, once it approaches 100 miles an hour, it'll blow the fuses because the scanners can't turn into the wind. In freezing spray that hit all the windows I can't look out of them so just for the winter, I've put in a 1500-watt heater with a Clear View screen just so we can see where we're going.

In the approach at Douglas Channel, the weather can get very, very cold. I don't know what this does to compound problems but I have seen, sitting in Old Town hunting, where it's well in excess of 30 below zero, winds blowing 70-80 miles-an-hour, 25-30 foot sea running and sea smoke 100 feet in the air so you have no visual on ground level.

I have no idea how big a towboat you need or whatever to maintain steerage of those large ships in those bodies of water with a 25-30 foot sea running and no visibility at water ground zero.

I think to transit mainland inlets in that part of the B.C. coast in the winter time is just asking when something might happen; it's not "if" at all. And that would be absolutely, totally devastating.

## BROADSIDE

### Milan Stanga

*North Coast*

If you had 100 or 150-kilometre winds and they hit the broadside of a supertanker, the tugs would not be moving the supertanker. The supertanker would be pulling the tugs.

## SMOKED SALMON PIZZAS

### Mae Jong-Bowles

*Great for appetizers.*

1 (30cm) prepared thin crust pizza shell

¼ C sour cream

juice of ½ lemon

2 T fresh dill leaves, chopped or snipped

150 g smoked salmon, thinly sliced

¼ cucumber, thinly sliced

¼ red onion, finely chopped

3 T capers, drained

Preheat the oven to 400° F. Crisp the pizza crust for 5 minutes on a perforated pizza pan or on an oven shelf.

Meanwhile, mix the sour cream, lemon juice and dill in a small bowl.

Remove the pizza shell from the oven and leave to stand until cool to the touch.

Once cooled, spread on the sour cream-dill sauce and evenly spread the sliced smoked salmon to the edges. Top the pizza with sliced cucumber, red onion, and capers, cut and serve.

### Sherri Bury – second recipe

250 g cream cheese

2 T horseradish

½ C or more minced purple onion

½ t dried dill

capers

smoked salmon

Brown a thin crust pizza shell for 10 minutes.

Mix the cream cheese and horseradish with the dill and half the purple onion. Spread over shell. Cover with thin sliced smoked salmon, the rest of the minced purple onion and more dill. Sprinkle capers over the top.

Slice into small wedges and chill in the fridge. Can be done ahead of time.

WILD WINDS

Photo: Mae Jong-Bowles

## EXCESSIVE WIND

### Shannon Vanderheide

*Prince Rupert*

In the last two years, there have been two accidents that I know about involving freighters in this harbour with assisting tugs. In one instance, a freighter hit the beach at the grain terminal with tugs assisting while trying to dock a ship. This was a brand new freighter picking up its first load.

The second incident took place at the coal terminal with a coal freighter. The assisting tug ended up being ran over sideways by the freighter and the bow of the tug went into the propeller of the freighter, nearly sinking the tug and rendering the freighter and tug useless until extensive repairs were completed to both vessels.

Both of these freighters' size pales in comparison to the size of the supertankers Enbridge is proposing.

One of the main factors in both of these freighter accidents was weather; sudden excessive wind at the wrong time, not mechanical error.

## TANKERS CAN'T SHELTER

### Warren Nelson, Ama gydem naat

*Kitkatla, Gitxaala*

With how rough it is through our channels, we're able to turn back, to come back home or go get shelter somewhere, but these big tankers will not be able to turn around and find shelter in our channels.

# Salmon and Feta Cheese Pie

Luanne Roth

1½ C light cottage cheese

3 large eggs

3 t of fresh dill, chopped fine

¼ t of pepper

half pint jar of canned pink or sockeye salmon (or a 213 gm tin) or a cup of cooked wild salmon

1/3 C feta cheese

4 chopped green onions

9-inch deep dish pie crust (thaw while preparing)

Preheat oven to 375° F.

Blend cottage cheese until smooth. Add eggs, dill and pepper and blend.

Break up the drained salmon and feta cheese: add them and the green onion to the cheese and egg mixture. Stir and pour into the pie crust.

Bake for 40 minutes until pie is firmly set.

This pie can be served warm or at room temperature. Take it to a potluck. Serve with salad.

Photo: Michael Ambach

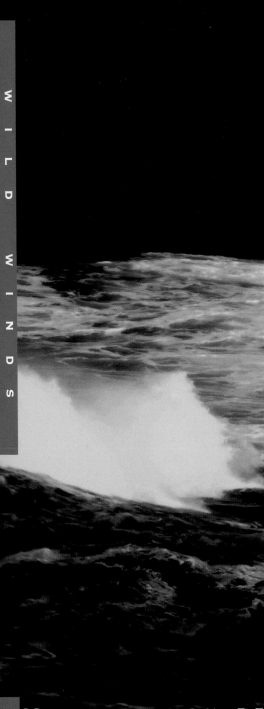

## VOLLEYBALL TRIP

### Richard Audet

*Prince Rupert*

I coached volleyball and basketball and on one of our first trips to volleyball we had to go to Prince Rupert, and you could take a float plane, but that cost too much money to raise; so we took a gillnetter. We rented a gillnetter to go to Prince Rupert. And on the way back we got caught in a storm, and I didn't know storms could be like this.

I thought I was going to die. The water -- the waves were bigger -- I couldn't see the waves really because they were bigger than the boat and I just knew that the waves were coming completely over the boat and we were going up and down. And even the kids who really knew the ocean, they were a little scared, and one of them made his way over to me and he said, you know, "Hey, Audet, if we die, it's your fault."

And I'm telling you this story because I know the future of this wild coast is in your hands, and when you make your decision about whether 200 or so supertankers should go through these straits, these rocky narrow passages, keep in mind the extreme weather that can happen on very short notice.

*The stillness between tides and winds.*
*Snow blows through the emptiness*
*where my thoughts have been.*

# SANGAN RIVER MEDITATION

Susan Musgrave

*Haida Gwaii*

Photo: Moyna MacIlroy

Photo: Yvonne Collins

W
I
L
D

W
I
N
D
S

Photo/Michael Ambach

FOOD SECURITY

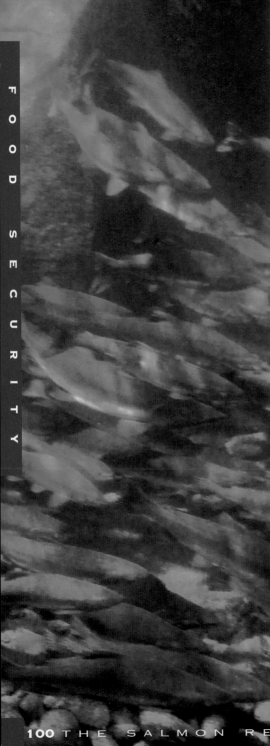

## PLASTIC BARRIERS

### Luanne Roth

*Prince Rupert*

On a holiday traveling down from the north coast with my trunk full of salmon for relatives, we passed a lot of highway construction south of Prince George. All along the road we'd see these funny irregular draped plastic structures along the ditches amongst the heavy machinery and piles of crush. What the heck?

I finally twigged that those ditches are little streams: part of the Fraser river system; nursing grounds of wild salmon. The salmon eggs in the gravel need to breath; to take oxygen from our beautiful pristine stream waters. Without those plastic barriers even a little mud washed into the water will settle on the eggs and suffocate them. We truly care here in BC, about the millions of wild salmon which travel hundreds of miles inland and fill the province's waters with life.

## COHO EVERYWHERE

### Keith Isherwood

*Prince Rupert*

I put in the waterline for the salmon enhancement facility in Oona River. It was part of a stream inventory program where we were examining and taking data on the habitat and the DNA samples of the coho salmon between here and the Kasiks River.

To my delight, just about every little bit of water has coho in it. A habitat as big as this table, would have juvenile coho in it everywhere. And I can't see how you can put a pipeline in without utterly destroying these little bits. And every little fish counts. You know, they don't all spawn in the big main channel they need every little piece to exist.

We have coho running through our golf course; they're everywhere and that's just the coho. There are several other salmon species that are seriously important to us. That's where our money comes from. This town was built for fishing.

## SALMON FILLETS WITH WASABI SAUCE

Karen McKinster

¼ C chopped onion

I T grated ginger

I C water

3-4 T soy sauce

I salmon fillet or steaks

I t wasabi paste

¼ C mayo

¼ C yogurt

Heat oven to 400°F.

Combine ginger, onion, water & soy sauce in a baking dish. Add fillet, skin side down and spoon a little onion/ginger mixture over it. Bake until opaque about 15 min.

Mix mayo, yogurt and wasabi dressing together. Drizzle dressing over the fish to serve.

Photo: Michael Ambach

FOOD SECURITY

Photo: Moyna MacIlroy

## ROMANCE

Henry Clifton,
Gnulx Hyitk

*Prince Rupert*

We have a romance with the waters and the land, and we're the most eco-friendly people in the world. We don't have certificates to prove it, but we prove it by how much we love the land, how much we protect and look after it.

I was brought up First Nations and, I guess it comes that way first, but you hear the passion from a non-First Nations and he lives out on the water.

We go out and we travel around out there, you know, looking for fish, put out our lines. We take what nature gives us, we take it home. And we provide other people with the fish.

## BOAT BUILDING IN OLD MASSETT

Oliver Bell,
Gliii glaa,
(Calm Sea)

*Haida Gwaii*

It was amazing how boat building and fishing supported so many families.

In Old Massett the Davidsons built a boat called "The Davidson Girl". "The Haida Warrior" was built by the Whites. "The Bennett" was built by the Bennetts. "The May Queen" was built by Joe Edgars. "Haida Brave" was built by Andrew York. "The Gwen Rose" was built by the Jones. Just to name a few.

Photo: Michael Ambach

*Much of the old locally built wooden fleet has been replaced with modern aluminum or fibreglass seiners, gillnetters and trollers but this picture shows the Legacy in the background. Still fishing, it is the last Wahl boat, built across the harbour from Prince Rupert.*

## GUIDE'S SPECIAL

### Noel Gyger, local guide

*"You meet the nicest people on the river banks."*

salmon

mayo

sour cream

dill weed

hot Tabasco sauce

Skin and de-bone salmon. Cut into small chunks and put in baking dish. Mix equal portions of mayo and sour cream. Add some dill weed and shake in hot Tabasco sauce. Pour mixture over the fish chunks and bake.

Photo: Moyra MacIlroy

Photo: Yvonne Collins

FOOD SECURITY

FOOD SECURITY

## HOW INDEPENDENT WE ARE

### Chief Clarence Nelson, Nestoix (Grandfather of a Handshake)

*Metlakatla*

Many visiting people in the commercial sector and many of my uncles trolled there (just north of the Skeena). It's close to home. I made a commercial living trolling along those islands, along Stephens all the way down to catch the huge spring salmon that were bound back for the Skeena River— the coho, and all the species that come in. That place had so much importance for us, culturally, and it provided us our food security. Later on in life it provided us with the economic opportunity to make a living by fishing.

In 1862 we, the Metlakatla people, had our own cannery. It was the first commercial cannery to process our resources. It helped sustain our community. We didn't have to have government hand-outs. That's how independent we are and that's how we were taught. We're gifted. Our grandparents are gifted with music. My grandfather was a concert band leader. We enjoyed all of these things. It kind of is the entertainment we share with one another. We did everything, we built schools, we built canneries, we built homes, we built churches and had our own police force.

## YEAR OF THE DOG

### Rick Hoagan

*Prince Rupert*

"Rick, what does your jacket mean?"

Oh, my crew has a thing. Like I say, 2009 was the largest pink salmon run in that part of the world. Not last year, the year before, we had the largest sockeye return in over a hundred years, so I got the crew a jacket that said: "Year of the Sockeye" because we broke records.

This year, it's "Year of the Dog". My largest production of dog salmon ever was in 1973 and I produced 350,000 lbs. of chum salmon. This fall (2011), I put in 550,000 lbs. of chum salmon.

That's the significance of the jacket.

# MARINER'S STEW

## Sarah Chi Brown

*This recipe is named for the littlest mariner in our family; Maren Dorine.*

6 T olive oil

1 or 2 large onions

3 stalks of celery

2 C sliced mushrooms

1 large can tomatoes

salt and pepper

pinch of thyme

1½ C water or potato water

2 lbs whitefish or salmon, filleted, cut in large chunks, bones removed

½ C white wine

2 T chopped parsley

Heat the oil in a large pan or wok. Add the onions and cook until they look translucent. Add the vegetables and mushrooms until the mushrooms are nicely browned. Add the tomatoes and seasonings. Add the water and simmer about 30 minutes. Add the fish and wine and cook until the fish flakes easily. Add the parsley and stir. Serve.

*Variation:* Add shellfish.

Photo: Moyna MacIlroy

## RUPERT AT THE MOUTH OF THE SKEENA RIVER

Rick Haugan

*Prince Rupert*

I'm fourth generation fishing out of Prince Rupert. My family started fishing here over a hundred years ago. My great grandfather brought a steam trawler from Grimsby, England, down around the horn, before Panama, came up the Hecate Strait and had to wait for them to build a cold storage so they could start fishing into Rupert.

Rupert at the mouth of the Skeena River is near the Alaska border. Just south is an area of channels and islands in the entrance to Douglas Channel, which, contrary to public belief is a very healthy salmon area.

In 2009, there were 6.6 million pink salmon taken there by the seine fleet. That's an all- time record. That's 300,000 bigger than the previous written history of that area.

These salmon stocks, like all Pacific Coast salmon, are right-turning fish. They go out in the ocean, they come up and they come down from the Alaska panhandle. Just seaward of the Port of Prince Rupert is the approach area for most of the fish originating in those waters. They'll landfall probably between Stephens Island and Banks Island. They'll be feeding in through Otter Channel, Squally Channel, Lewis Pass, and Wales Channel proper.

That's their main migration route and if you overlap that on a map with the proposed route of the tankers, it's the exact same route; there's no difference at all.

## SUSTENANCE

Conrad Lewis

*Prince Rupert*

Sustenance is a word that always comes to my mind, but when it's commercialized we'll have to change sustenance to making a living.

I have an ancestral line to this region that goes far beyond 1,000 years. But we weren't all Prince Rupertites. We weren't all here 20, 50, 1,000 years ago. We're transients. We came here because of an industry overwhelming with wealth and prosperity and all these kinds of great things.

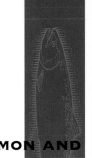

## SALMON AND BROCCOLI QUICHE

### Norma Leakey

2/3 C cheddar cheese

1½ C cooked or canned salmon

2/3 C chopped onion

1 C broccoli, green peas or preferred vegetables

1 1/3 C milk

3 eggs

¼ tsp salt

¼ tsp pepper

Coarsely chop the cheese and save half a cup for the top. Put the cheese with the salmon and vegetables in a bowl. Mix the milk, eggs, salt and pepper in a blender then pour it in to the vegetables, cheese and salmon. Mix it all up and pour into your quiche dish. It's crustless. Add the remaining cheddar to the top.

Cook at 400° F for 30-40 minutes or until a knife inserted into the middle comes out clean.

Photo: Michael Ambach

FOOD SECURITY

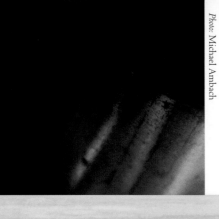

Photo: Michael Ambach

## SHARED WITH THE WORLD

### Conrad Lewis

*Prince Rupert*

So when we get into the production of this fish, when we produce a commodity, a shared commodity, not with Prince Rupert, not with British Columbia, not with Canada, but with the world and we have our labels pasted on cans that we produce in the very same plants that exist right to this day, down the street; there's pride in that.

Photo: Moyna MacIlroy

## GOING SOUTH

### Reg Davidson, Skil kaatl'aas (Spirit Weath who is rising), Hlk 'yaan K'ustaan Sgaanuwee (Frog Spirit) and Kiidlajuuwee (the bow of the canoe that cuts the water in half)

*Old Massett*

We all love this area. When I talk about Langara, it's quite scary because every fish that's going south goes past Langara. When I go fishing for sockeye there in August, I'm catching Fraser River sockeye. If I'm trolling at Cape— at Shag Rock, I'm catching a fish that goes to the Columbia. If I'm fishing down the west side, I'm catching sockeye that goes down to the Fraser River or I'm catching fish that goes all the way to Vancouver Island.

Any fish that's going south goes around our island and it's quite scary when you're dealing with a tanker that's bigger than our village, carrying oil.

## PANKO CRUSTED SALMON FISHCAKES

### Yvonne Collins

½ pint jar of traditional aboriginal canned smoked salmon.

½ pint jar regular sockeye salmon

6 C mashed potatoes

I C finely chopped carrots

I C finely chopped celery

1/3 C finely minced chives

I small onion finely minced

3 eggs

salt and pepper to taste

Panko crumbs

light cooking oil.

Mix salmon and all ingredients leaving one beaten egg for coating. (If all you have is regular canned sockeye use 2 tins) Form into patties. Dip into one beaten egg, then into Panko crumbs. Fry in pan with light oil coating.

These can be eaten hot, warm or cold. They can be frozen for later.

Serve with dips or sauces like Cajun or chili.

*Photo: Yvonne Collins*

## THE IMPACT

### Chief Clarence Nelson, Nestoix (Grandfather of a Handshake)

*Metlakatla*

In 2005 I had the honour and privilege of going up to Alaska as a hereditary person to meet with the First Nations people in southeast Alaska, up to Anchorage, to hear their stories of the impact of the Exxon Valdez oil spill. It was very touching, very moving to hear how they are suffering because they have lost their staple foods.

## EIGHTY THOUSAND VISITORS AND TEN MILLION SALMON

### Luanne Roth

*Prince Rupert*

One fall a few years ago we were down south visiting after the fishing season. Neither John's brother's family nor we had ever seen the famed millions strong Adams River sockeye run and the timing was right so off we went. Down a dusty gravel road in south central BC out in the country far from any city we found ourselves in a huge makeshift parking lot in a field.

We joined a crowd funneling along a riverside path. The procession was about eight or ten people wide, slow and happy, visiting along the way. Going in both directions were families with children and aging couples with canes. I was surprised to see groups of trendy teenagers out with their friends and a crowd I recognized was out taking a break from Robson Street weekdays in Vancouver. Here we were all wending our way. We stopped with awe whenever we could see the thousands of red sockeye crowding the river as we crowded the river bank. I later heard there were eighty thousand visitors over the few weekends and more than ten million salmon.

Even with the crowd there was time and room to stop and watch a female make a shallow scoop in the gravel. There was time to watch different suitors approach their choice, do a water dance of forward and back, round and round, and be accepted or rejected…time to witness the quick flurry of egg laying and darting fertilization. There was time to watch a tired spawned out salmon fin its tail and move up against the gentle current one last time before it lay still and drifted slowly, bumping along the gravel downstream.

*Pink Salmon Photo: Moyna MacIlroy*

# THREE PEPPER LOAF

### John Rowlands

I 213 g tin sockeye salmon

I 213 g tin pink salmon

I egg

½ C bread crumbs

¼ C minced onion

½ C combined mixed orange, red, and yellow peppers, minced

mixed fresh herbs:

I T chopped oregano

I T chopped tarragon

I T chopped parsley

dash of pepper

Drain salmon. Discard bones. Mash salmon. Add egg and bread crumbs. Mix in peppers, onion, and fresh herbs. Blend until smooth, adding more bread crumbs if necessary to shape into a bread like loaf.

Place loaf on a parchment lined cookie sheet. Bake at 350 F for approximately 45 minutes until the top is firm and golden. At this stage, you can glaze it by brushing on some bottled sweet chili sauce, or your favourite barbeque sauce, and bake for an additional 5 minutes.

Let the loaf cool, and then slice it up and serve with rice and your favourite vegetables.

It is also good served cold. Serves 4 people.

Note: Some folks add a bit of cooked yam to loaf.

## WE'VE LIVED OFF THE OCEANS FOR THOUSANDS OF YEARS

**Allan Davidson, Guskin (Seagulls Diving for Fish)**

*Haida Gwaii*

When I left home to go to university, I studied anthropology. I was in my third year, when one of my friends called me and said there was an opening doing some archaeology fieldwork back home, on Haida Gwaii.

In 2002, we bottomed out, we hit sterile beach sand, and when we hit the bottom, I climbed into a 2x2 excavation unit, and standing there...I got chills on the back of my neck and my hair stood up. To be on the ground that my ancestors stood on 10,700 years ago; I could just feel their power.

I have worked on many other sites— Rose Spit is the most recent at about 600 years old. At all of these sites there are fish bones, there are clam shells, and shellfish...So as the previous speakers have stated, and from what I know as a Haida living here and working as an archaeologist here, our people and our culture have survived off the lands and oceans of Haida Gwaii for thousands of years.

## BRIGHT FUTURE

**Joy Thorkelson**

*Prince Rupert*

We've heard that the well-being of the environment is linked to the well-being of the fish, which is linked to the well-being of our communities.

We have a bright future. But it is only a bright future if we continue to have fish. And we will only continue to have fish if we have an environment that supports fish.

Photo: Michael Ambach

# Steamed Salmon with Huckleberries

### Eileen Nelson

*My Auntie Da'a taught me this recipe when I was a child at our summer camp on Dundas Island.*

whole cleaned salmon

skunk cabbage leaves

huckleberries
(or wild blueberries)

Cut the stem out of the bottom of the skunk cabbage leaves. Wash them very well with salt water, being careful to wash in all the grooves. Put a handful or so of huckleberries inside the salmon and roll and tuck it up in the leaves.

Cook it placed close to a smoldering campfire. Turn it several times and let it steam until cooked. The skunk cabbage leaves are not eaten just the berry flavoured salmon.

Photo: Ken McCormick

## Get Half a Gram a Day

The recommended intake of Omega-3 by the American Heart Association (AHA), World Health Organization (WHO), European Food Safety Authority and many other agencies, for cardio-protective effects in adults without coronary heart disease (CHD), is 0.5 g daily. (Ikonomou et al 2007) 1.0 g daily of Omega-3 is often recommended for individuals with CHD.

There is mounting evidence that eating even only half the daily recommended amount of Omega-3 has many general health benefits: decrease in depression, enhancement of cognitive and visual abilities, prevention of cancer and even improved love life. But perhaps the best studied is the efficacy of Omega-3 as a preventative of death by coronary heart disease (CHD). It is estimated that daily intake of only 1/4 gram of Omega-3/day over a 70-year lifetime would result in 7125 fewer CHD deaths per 100,000 individuals. (Mozaffarian and Rimm 2006)

### Ocean Caught Skeena Sockeye are Highly Prized

Our cold water fish are prized around the world for their exceptionally rich Omega-3 content. These local waters provide millions of servings for Canadians. Even a few servings a year of omega-3 rich wild fish have significant health benefits.

BC has some of the highest quality salmon in the world. Salmon connoisseurs know where their fish come from. Generally wild salmon are valued for their oil content.

Salmon store up oil reserves for their long migrations. The salmon with the longest migrations generally have the highest oil content. Once they stop eating out at sea they start using up their reserves. The oil stored in the muscle/fillet is depleted first.

The main Skeena sockeye run heading to Babine Lake far inland has a very high oil content when caught in the ocean. PRES tested 126 ocean caught Skeena area sockeye in 2012 and their average fat content (skin off fillet) was a whopping 11.5%! The USDA average for raw sockeye is only 5.6%. (www.nal.usda.gov/fnic/foodcomp/search Accessed 9/21/12)

About one fifth of salmon oil is Omega- 3 so if that holds true for Skeena sockeye - 11.5% total oil would translate to 2.3 gm of Omega-3 oil per 100 gm serving.

Photo: May Jong-Bowles

**The world relies on wild captured fish from our oceans for global food security.**

The annual catch has stabilized around 80 billion kg. (FAO) That is about 10 kg for every person. The ocean provides crucial proteins, vitamins and oils to families around the world – we need fish for global food security.

In BC the total annual catch is about 200 million kg of wild seafood. This is a key component of Canadian food and nutritional security.

## Sustainable Fisheries

In the spring hundreds of millions of little salmon smolts come out from the rivers and streams to feed along the ocean shore. Huge schools can be seen down at the docks and under boats. Kayakers in the inlets or along the coast see the smolts around kelp and near shore. Skeena sockeye returns alone were about 2 million in 2011 and look even better in 2012. There are millions of pinks. There are Nass sockeye.

BC's salmon returns are millions strong. Much attention is focused, as it should be, on individual runs which are stocks of concern, but we shouldn't lose sight of the wealth of runs which number in the thousands, tens of thousands, hundreds of thousands and millions.

Our fishery is sustainable. The historical First Nations salmon catches analyzed around this region were comparable in magnitude to the average yearly commercial catch between 1901 and 2000. (Campbell, S. K., and V. L. Butler 2010)

## Selective Fishing

The north coast salmon fisheries are closely managed. Sometimes a large abundant run is co-mingled with a weaker one. In order to avoid over fishing of weak stocks, daily test fisheries are conducted and analyzed. Opening times and areas are carefully chosen. Additional selective fishing techniques such as: daylight sets, weed-lines, mesh size specifications, short set times, short nets, recovery boxes, and brailing are used to reduce the pressure on weaker salmon runs. Once the total allowable number of fish from a weak run has been caught, the ocean fishery is closed whether or not there is still an abundance of the stronger co-mingled run.

Terminal fisheries are also selective. However after their long migration upriver, Skeena sockeye which started out with over 11.5 % fat content in the ocean, end up at Babine Lake terminal fishery, with the fat content of their skin-off fillets depleted to only 2.0% — a tragic loss of human nutrition. There are strategies to respect First Nations rights and maximize ocean selectivity and nutrition which can benefit from increased local input into fisheries management and build on the good relations of coastal and upriver First Nations in the north.

## North Coast Commercial Salmon Fishing Fleet

The salmon fishery is very important to the Norwegians, Swedes, Scots and other pioneers who catch salmon for Canadians. But the First Nations deserve special recognition. Consider that First Nations people make up only 3.5% of the population in BC, yet they make up, as individuals, roughly one half of the commercial salmon fishing fleet in the north coast and 30% in BC. (Michelle James 2003). The salmon fishing industry is crucial to their coastal villages and to Prince Rupert, nestled at the mouth of the Skeena River, where many First Nations people and pioneers have settled over the last century to work in the industry.

The Exxon-Valdez tanker spill in Prince Williams Sound, Alaska is a warning for us. Many of the fisheries in that area are still not reopened more than twenty years later.

One of the tankers proposed for our coast would hold almost ten times the oil which spilt from the Exxon Valdez.

In the Prince William Sound, the area affected by the Valdez oil spill stretched a distance equal to about 75% the length of BC's coast. The Exxon Valdez only spilled about 40 million liters of its oil.

Just one single oil tanker proposed for BC can carry over 300 million liters. This is getting close to half the entire amount of oil which spilled in the Gulf disaster — a disaster which affected five states. 800 million liters of oil spilled in the Gulf BP spill.

In other parts of the world, governments and the oil industry have offered to designate and fund marine parks in return for the public's acceptance of oil tankers or offshore drilling. As we saw in the BP Gulf oil spill, designating an area as a marine park will not protect its birds and beaches from oil.

APPENDIX

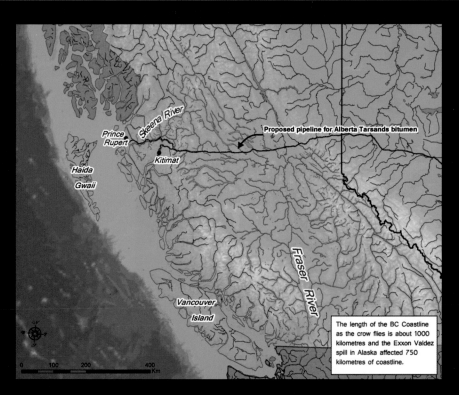

Proposed pipeline for Alberta Tarsands bitumen

Prince Rupert

Skeena River

Kitimat

Haida Gwaii

Fraser River

Vancouver Island

The length of the BC Coastline as the crow flies is about 1000 kilometres and the Exxon Valdez spill in Alaska affected 750 kilometres of coastline.

0   100   200   400 Km

BC Map showing Proposed Pipeline with the Two Marine Terminal Alternatives:
Kitimat at the end of Douglas Channel or Prince Rupert at the mouth of the Skeena River

Craig Outhet/ Strait Geomatics

Data sources: *Province of BC, National Oceanic and Atmospheric Administration &*
*Enbridge Northern Gateway application-"Marine Terminal Alternatives"*

## About the Prince Rupert Environmental Society (PRES)

PRES is a non-profit society which was founded in 1989 as the *Prince Rupert Recycling Society* and helped establish the recycling depot now run by Skeena Queen Charlotte Regional District. PRES expanded its mandate and worked on streamkeeping and other issues.

In 2003 there was a proposal to put ten open-netcage fishfarms into the Skeena estuary. PRES launched its *Save our Skeena Salmon Campaign* with maps, articles, a website, petitions, billboards, a video we helped produce (directed by Twyla Roscovich - *Call from a Coast*) and more. In March 2008 we won a north coast moratorium on fishfarms.

Now four years later, we are working to protect our area from a new threat — oil tankers.